The Yummy Marriage

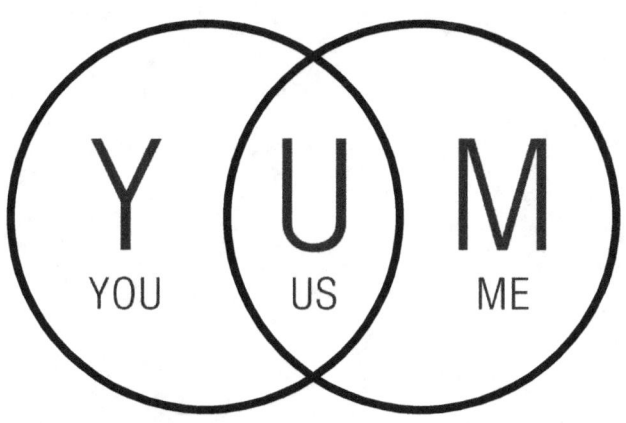

**Tools and Insights From
The Acclaimed Marriage Quest Program**

Cathie W. Helfand
with Dr. Israel Helfand

Copyright © 2021 by Cathleen W. Helfand.

All rights reserved. This book or any portion thereof may not be reproduced or used in any manner whatsoever without the express written permission of the author except for the use of brief quotations in a book review.

Printed in the United States of America
First Printing, 2021

ISBN: 978-1-64704-317-9 (Paperback)

For my father,
Jurgen "Jerry" Worthing.
There would be no Marriage Quest Retreats
if it were not for his tireless efforts
and the love and faith he had in our work.

Contents

Preface VII

Chapter 1: The YUMMY Marriage 1
Chapter 2: The Journey of Marriage 13
Chapter 3: Love, Love, Love 26
Chapter 4: Trouble in Paradise 34
Chapter 5: A Healthy Foundation 45
Chapter 6: Communication 101 56
Chapter 7: Sex and Sexploration 75
Chapter 8: Affairs and Infidelity 93
Chapter 9: Divorce 101
Chapter 10: Parenthood and Marriage 111
Chapter 11: Becoming a YUMMY Person 118
Chapter 12: Religion and Spirituality 136
Appendix 1: More About Cathie 145
Appendix 2: More About Israel 147
Appendix 3: Conversation Starters 149
Appendix 4: Recipes for Family Living 151
Appendix 5: A Story of Spirituality 157
Appendix 6: Books and Other Resources 159

Acknowledgements 169

Preface

Why a "YUMMY" Marriage?

I PICKED THE name "The *YUMMY* Marriage," or I suppose it picked me, after many clients commented on how they related to my Venn diagram of "Y-U-M".

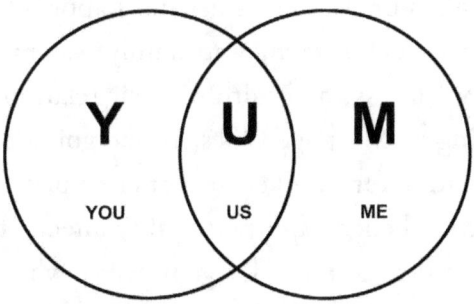

Often, couples want to be stronger as individuals, and they want to have a bigger and stronger "we" or "us" together. That is the secret recipe for a healthy marriage—a strong and healthy "you" combined with a strong and healthy "me" to create the best possible "us." YUM!

PREFACE

Marriage Quest

Israel and I are a married couple who have been working together as Marriage Counselors and Sex Therapists since the early '80s. Like any couple, we have had our own ups and downs. We know about the benefits and values of a committed relationship as well as the challenges of juggling a marriage while staying true to our individual selves.

Together we run a world-famous retreat program at our homestead in Northern Vermont called Marriage Quest. We work with one couple at a time, focusing on their specific issues and goals. Most couples come to us during a crisis to make a decision about their marriage. They are often on the edge of a divorce, usually after an affair. They are angry and frustrated with their spouse. They usually feel helpless and hopeless about their situation and their future together.

For many of these couples, getting a divorce seems like the only solution to their power struggles and emotional pain. They usually think that their differences are irreconcilable and that they are not compatible. Typically, they do not see a better solution. We are their last resort.

Like highly-skilled physicians, Israel and I apply our knowledge and experience in marriage counseling and family systems theories to do a "marital triage." We assess the health of their relationship and of each individual. Coming to Marriage Quest is like going to the Emergency Room for an evaluation for a broken arm or chest pain. We examine how each person's history, beliefs, and personality affects their relationship. Then, we explore critical issues and urgent needs, while applying proven techniques to heal wounds and create a healthy path forward.

Marriage Today

The institution of marriage is in a state of rebalancing today. People are living longer than ever before, yet stress abounds. Many people are choosing to stay single. Some are choosing to live in group situations or in polyamorous relationships. Do newlyweds really expect to stay married to the same person for 50 years, or has divorce and remarriage become the future pattern? Many millennials are choosing to live together without getting married. Is that a new norm too?

Only half of new marriages will last a lifetime, research says. The odds of staying married improve with education, financial stability, and age. Yet, only 20% of those surviving marriages report that both spouses are truly happy in their marriage. Israel calls these "The 20%." I call them the "The YUMMY Couples."

We all want to be part of a YUMMY couple. Most of us can be, with a little work. Whether you are a married couple dealing with an affair or betrayal, a husband and wife who feel more like roommates, or a newly-engaged couple looking to strengthen the foundation of your marriage, the lessons in this book can help you.

More than 75% of the distressed couples that work with us turn their relationship around. They eliminate old beliefs and learn new strategies to stabilize their relationship—and then tools to spice it up. They survive, and then they thrive. They leave with a deep understanding of their relationship, practical tools for maintaining and enhancing it, and a great hope for the future, together.

Inviting You to Our Table

The tips and techniques presented in this book have come from over 35 years as professional marriage counselors as well as from our life as a married couple. This is our way of bringing the Marriage Quest lessons to you in your home. You and your partner can learn the skills. You'll create recipes for your personal and marital success, become healthy role models for your children, and serve up a sweeter, YUMMIER life together.

An intimate committed relationship, whether legally sanctioned or not, is one of the most difficult relationships of all. The ups and downs and emotional intensity can challenge you on a very deep level. You may feel intense feelings that you haven't experienced before.

PREFACE

This book is for anyone who is interested in understanding and improving their significant intimate relationship. You can learn to be happier and healthier as an individual and as a couple. There are specific things you can do to increase your chances of surviving and thriving as friends and lovers. This book contains many ideas and tools to show you how to improve yourself, your life, your family, and your marriage.

Our work focuses on married and non-married heterosexual couples, who are typically looking to be monogamous. Yet many of the lessons here can be applied to any intimate relationship, whether gay or straight, monogamous, or polyamorous. You may even find them useful for dealing with your friends, colleagues, children, or parents.

There are "YUMMY Food for Thought" prompts throughout this book to help you explore on your own or with your partner. In addition, there are blank pages at the end of this book for you to write some notes, collect your thoughts, or process your feelings.

You, too, can be part of the 20%.
You, too, can have a YUMMY marriage.
And we can help!

Chapter 1

The YUMMY Marriage

ISRAEL AND I met in the fall of 1979 in graduate school at the University of Bridgeport in Connecticut. We remember the details differently, but we both agree we had an instant connection—instant chemistry. There was only one slight complication to our infatuation: we were both married at that time, to other people.

Ooops!

We remained friends for several years. Once we were both divorced, we found our way back to each other and embarked on a committed relationship together.

We were happy and in love. We were inseparable. We did everything together. We were best friends and great lovers. We were couple-centered. We seemed indestructible and bulletproof.

Our Wedding

Then, life got very busy, very quickly. In three short years we started our counseling business, remodeled an old house for our office space, got married, had a baby, and turned our tiny log cabin into a home for our growing family.

When our son David was born, everything changed. David stole my heart. I felt love for him in a deep, new, and powerful way that I had never felt before. Suddenly, I was putting all of my time, energy, love, and attention onto our son, leaving little for my husband.

While I was consumed by our baby, Israel was consumed by his work. He was going to the office a lot. Some days he went without me and some days he stayed late to do paperwork. Our little counseling center grew in leaps and bounds and quickly became very successful.

When David was about one and a half years old, Israel came to me and told me that he was getting nervous. Women were starting to come onto him, flashing their panties, and making suggestive comments. He missed me, and was becoming very tempted.

OH SHIT!

Let's just say that was a rough week. We talked and cried together for many hours. Although it was tough at the time, this crisis put us onto a better path. We talked more frequently—and on a deeper level. We discussed what we each needed from the other person. We began spending more time together, laughing and having fun. We started to enjoy each other again like we had in the very beginning of our relationship.

Many years later I realized something: Israel was really brave in coming to me, and I was very lucky. Many spouses don't have the courage to speak up when they are unhappy or feeling unfulfilled in their marriage.

Instead, they do stupid things like over-eating, over-drinking, spending too much money, or having an affair. Because Israel was brave enough to be vulnerable and honest, we had the opportunity to fix things before trust was broken and our marriage was even more challenged.

So, What is a YUMMY Marriage?

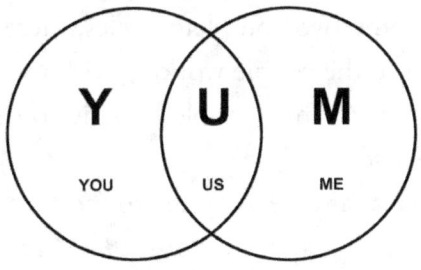

In a healthy marriage there is: **You**, **Us** and **Me**. I call this recipe: **YUM**.

A **YUMMY** marriage is where each person is:

- Comfortable in their own skin
- Aware of their own strengths and weaknesses
- Flexible and tolerant
- Able to navigate challenging topics with compassion and empathy, while having personal strength and conviction

In a YUMMY marriage there is give-and-take. The partners are able to cooperate with each other, so there's a sense of teamwork. They have hobbies and interests in common, and each have personal interests that are not practiced together.

Each person encourages their spouse to talk about their life adventures and dreams for the future. They spend time listening to each other's stories. They have a life together as well as having some separate activities.

YUMMY couples are able to negotiate serious conversations with positive outcomes. In addition to deep conversations YUMMY couples are able to get beyond life's seriousness and have fun together—to be playful and silly. They are able to celebrate their joy and happiness together. They are able to laugh together as well as cry together.

Two Whole People, One Healthy Couple

A YUMMY marriage is built on the intersection of two people. That means that the relationship starts with two strong, emotionally developed individuals. Without the two complete circles, there can be no overlap. Every week I explain to the couple working with us that they need to be two whole people, not two half people looking to complete themselves with a partner or spouse.

The language that many people use around love can be misleading. It may seem romantic to search for your *other half,* your *better half,* or your *soul mate,* but looking for a partner to complete you often leads to insecurities and relationship struggles later on.

An old friend of mine used to say, "insecurity is the root of all evil." I tend to agree. Certainly, loneliness and the search for a sense of completion and security in someone else can be majorly problematic.

When two people enter into a marriage, ideally, they each have a well-developed sense of self. This means having good self-awareness and good self-esteem. It means knowing the answers to questions like:

- What is important to you? What do you value?
- What do you want to achieve in your lifetime?

- What career or jobs fit your talents and desired lifestyle?
- How have your family background and other life experiences influenced you in positive ways? How have they influenced you in negative ways?
- How do your past childhood and relationship wounds affect how you respond to conflict and stress today?

Hopefully, you understand the answers to these questions and can discuss them with your partner while you are dating. Having open, honest conversations can help you decide if your values align, and if this is a person you want to share the rest of your life with. Understanding who you are and where you are headed is very useful. Everything gets more complicated when people commit to a marriage before developing a good sense of self.

It's important to note that self-awareness and maturity isn't always tied to age. Many people gain a stronger sense of self as they get older, but age is not the only indicator of maturity. There are many older people who seem mature in many ways but still have limited self-awareness, inadequate relationship skills, and a low self-esteem. Even if you started your relationship later in life, it is useful to re-evaluate yourself and your relationship from time to time. After all, you need to know yourself and love yourself before you can truly love another person.

From You and Me, Building Us

Having a solid sense of self is instrumental, but to have a YUMMY marriage you also need to focus on nurturing your bond with your partner. Today, we expect everything from our spouse: to be best friends, great lovers, and equal partners at home. That's a lot of pressure, so it can be hard to find just the right amount of dependence on each other.

Let's use the YUM symbols to consider three common relationship patterns: independent, dependent and interdependent.

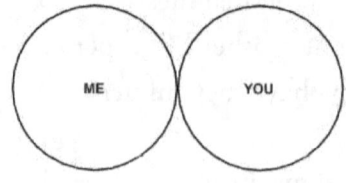

For **independent** people, the circles do not overlap at all. These partners do their own thing, exclusive of their spouse. Their lives do not intersect much at all. These people have separate circles of friends, and clearly are at risk of being attracted to new lovers and eventually separating and divorcing.

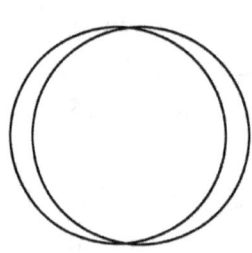

Overly **dependent** people, sometimes referred to as being codependent, rely on their spouse for everything. They cannot think for themselves. Typically, they are challenged in their self-awareness and have a low self-esteem. They lack the ability to speak up about their concerns or desires. They would benefit from a stronger and healthier sense of self and self-worth.

Despite the seeming closeness, people in dependent relationships are enmeshed. They often begin pushing each other away because of their overbearing connection. Dependent people are at risk for an affair because their lives are too intertwined and too close. They have no room for excitement, mystery, or surprises together because everything is known and predictable. So, they may seek that excitement and adventure elsewhere.

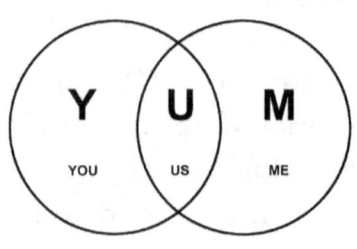

Inter-dependent people are our YUMMY spouses. They have a healthy balance of thinking and doing for themselves as well as relying on their spouse for some needs and wants. If there are children or pets, the partners work together harmoniously to address the needs of the family. They can be themselves and still be loved by their spouse.

Ebbs and Flows in Connection

We've just learned three types of relationship dynamics, but the truth is that most relationships ebb and flow, experiencing different levels of connection at different times. Most couples have experienced times when they felt bonded and connected as a couple—they felt as though they "were one" together.

This often occurs in the beginning of a love relationship, when you are falling in love and intoxicated with each other. It's the honeymoon, or limerence, phase of a relationship, when you are high on each other and on the dreams of what your relationship can become. Everything seems possible.

Over time, that feeling of unity might not be a constant presence, but still pops up in certain circumstances. Many couples feel this deep connection together during a session of passionate lovemaking. Other couples may experience that sense of bonding during the magical and spiritual birth of their child.

Feeling a deep connection is what bonds a couple together. It's needed for a long-term relationship. While bonding is essential to a committed relationship, couples that are overly close without enough space and individuality are in an unnatural state of enmeshment. No couple can stay in that state of oneness every minute of every day. That is unhealthy and unrealistic. Everyone needs some independence and space. Recognizing and accepting this is useful to becoming a successful YUMMY couple.

Although some couples are overly close, it's more common for couples to struggle to connect. This is the situation with most couples that come to work with us, and it is probably where you are right now. It might not be the healthiest time in your marriage, but it certainly is normal. This kind of disconnection happens at some time to almost all couples who have been married for many years.

Navigating Disconnection

Most of the couples who work with us are hoping to reconnect and rekindle their flame after drifting apart. Often there has been an emotional or sexual affair or other inappropriate relationships that threatened their marital bond. These couples are looking for that "in love" feeling again. Without it they are destined to separate and divorce.

An essential ingredient to satisfaction and success is to be couple-centered, not child-centered nor work-centered. Being couple-centered means that you make time to enjoy each other and that you turn to each other for support, guidance, and distraction from life's stressors.

Dividing and conquering can be a tactic for surviving the many demands of modern life. Sometimes it is unavoidable for many reasons, but nonetheless it is a dangerous threat to the well-being of the marriage. Often the wife becomes child-centered and the husband becomes work-centered. Unfortunately, they forget to focus on their relationship. This, in turn, leads to a disconnection.

Many disconnected couples experience:

- Poor communication
- Constant fighting
- Complete silence
- Lack of appreciation
- No fun time together
- Lack of affection
- No common interests
- Little to no sex, or an unsatisfying sex life

Feeling disconnected from your partner can be scary but it's entirely normal and expected during a long-term relationship. There are several predictable stages in a marriage with children when many couples feel stressed, distanced, and disconnected. The most common times include:

- The young child stage of parenthood, including pregnancy and childbirth. Husbands may feel abandoned because Mommy is dedicated to the young ones
- The turbulent teen years when rebellion is the norm
- The "empty nest" days when couples need to rediscover what they had in common before having their children

In addition, other circumstances can add additional stress and a sense of disconnect to a marriage. These include:

- Being long distance, navigating military deployment, or coping with frequent work travel
- When spouses are working opposite shifts or when a spouse has put their career on hold to be a full-time parent
- Navigating infertility, STIs, or some sexual dysfunction
- Taking care of an ill family member or grieving the death of a loved one
- Raising children with special needs

Sometimes, it's helpful just to acknowledge the disconnect that you're feeling and recognize that it's normal for this time in your life. From there, you can focus on remedying it and returning to a healthy interdependence and being a YUMMY couple.

Marriage and Family Systems

Marriage is an interconnected system. As systems-oriented therapists, that is how we view it. When Israel and I work with a couple, we have three "clients": the husband, the wife, and the marriage. Remember, YUM = you + us + me.

If there are any children, we want to consider them as well, because they are all part of the family system. We want to support the integrity of the entire system in seeking a new and healthier situation. More than any individual, your *relationship* is our client.

In traditional marriage counseling, the therapist will focus on one person more than the other. If someone had an affair or is destructive in the relationship, they are seen as the problem. They are often blamed for all of the issues in the marriage and family. They, in turn, will be called the "identified patient" and are usually diagnosed for insurance purposes.

In our young family, it was also obvious to me that Israel was the more aggressive person. It was clear to me that his "angry atmosphere" at times was definitely annoying and perhaps scary.

What wasn't obvious to me was that my passive nature contributed to our issues too. In some ways it was more damaging than his anger and frustration. It certainly was more confusing to the kids at times. They knew where Israel stood on matters but did not necessarily know what I was thinking or feeling or what I wanted. As I learned to use my voice and speak up more, Israel began to calm down, and our whole family system operated better.

Everyone is Responsible

Marriage is 100-100, not 50-50. That means that each partner should take 100% responsibility for making the marital relationship the best it can possibly be. You can be kind and loving even if your partner is grouchy or mean. If he or she does not respond well to your attempts at being nice, take a break and talk about it at a calmer time. Or, possibly seek some professional help.

Unfortunately, most couples know very well how to drag each other down. Ideally good marriage counseling should teach the couple how to stop that behavior, and instead help each spouse learn how to help raise the other up. The skills of positive communication and problem solving are key in knowing how to do this. Be responsible for yourself and for being a positive influence in your marriage. In a YUMMY marriage, spouses help each other feel good about themselves.

Challenges of Marriage

Marriage is like a mytho-poetic journey. In the story of *Seeking the Chalice* or *The Quest for the Holy Grail*, the knight in shining armor goes on a long sojourn. He does not take two steps to declare, "I found it. Here's the Chalice!" Instead, he faces many obstacles on his journey—dragons, demons, storms, and wars. It is a long adventure with many ups and downs.

In most marriages, couples have some good days and some bad days. Each person experiences great joy, as well as lots of pain and sorrow. It is not always smooth and effortless, so we should not expect it to be that way.

A marriage cannot always be as fun and easy as it was in the beginning. There will be obstacles along the way. I often say that a relationship is not a relationship until the couple has survived their first challenge. It is from the settling of disagreements that the relationship is solidified. What doesn't kill you really does make you stronger.

Couples need to understand that disagreements and conflict are inevitable. It is not the conflict that is the problem. It is how you deal with the conflict that will make or break your marriage. Your ability to communicate and negotiate your differences is most important. You'll learn how to do that as you progress through this book.

The only guarantee in life is that there will be change. People who are flexible, tolerant, and able to adapt well to change are happier, healthier, more grounded, and less depressed or anxious. These qualities can help you accept your differences with your partner, rather than blowing them out of proportion.

Like a broken bone that has been treated, a healed marriage is fortified. It may be more tender and sensitive, but nonetheless, it will be stronger.

Lighten Up!

Life can be very serious and stressful at times. "Terminal seriousness" is toxic to an intimate relationship. Your marriage should be a sanctuary—a refuge from life's storms. It should not be the cause of your stress. YUMMY couples find time for play, adventures, and FUN. A bit of well-timed humor and some playfulness can go a long way for you and for your marriage. So, lighten up and have some good ol' FUN!

Chapter 2

The Journey of Marriage

My parents were married in 1949 and were together for over 70 years. They taught me so much about love, marriage, and the value of a long-term commitment.

IF YOU THINK about marriage objectively, the whole thing seems a bit silly. You commit, usually early on in life, to spend the rest of your years, longer than you've been alive, with a person who you likely have only known for a year or two. And yet, people continue to get married and hope to stay married for a long time. What makes it work?

Knowing what to expect from your marriage and having a shared commitment to making it work go a long way in the success of a marriage. I call this a long-term committed marriage. It happens when both parties agree verbally or nonverbally that they are truly dedicated to each other for their lifetime. This is more than saying your vows—it's really believing in that commitment.

The beauty of making this kind of long-term commitment is that it allows each person the freedom to be themselves with less fear of losing their spouse. No one is walking on eggshells or hiding their true selves. Instead, the spouses know that they will work through their challenges and struggles together "no matter what."

A long-term marriage creates a safe environment to grow as individuals and to support each other with love and kindness, even on those days when you don't like each other very much.

The Institution of Marriage: A Little Background

Marriage is the most intimate relationship between two people, but it is also a ménage-a-trois between the couple, the government, and religious organizations. To understand how our society approaches marriage, it's helpful to know some history.

Marriage has been the basis for the family system for many years. Historically the need for coupling was based only on practical needs like survival, economics, and social or political advancement. Romantic ideals or individual desires weren't part of it. The concept of personal fulfillment and romantic love in marriage is relatively new to society.

The Modern American Marriage

The idea of marriage for love and fulfillment is linked closely with the American ideals of religious freedom and "the pursuit of happiness." Many immigrants came to America with romantic dreams and visions. For the first time in history, man's right to exist for his (or her) own personal happiness was politically recognized and supported.

Finally, men and women were more likely to marry someone of their own choosing based on the goal of happiness, friendship, and attraction. People could pursue personal and emotional fulfillment with each other. Couples were choosing their own mate without needing approval of their parents or other influential people.

The movement from farming to industry in the 1800s, known as the Industrial Revolution, completely changed the structure of the family. Families moved away from farming and hunting, distancing themselves from the large extended family and a community-based life. Instead, they focused on factory work, city life, and the nuclear family.

During this transition, couples became more independent; separating from their parents, grandparents, siblings, aunts, uncles, and cousins. Men became providers and wage earners, leaving the home in order to work. Women were no longer needed for their physical stamina and strength. They could now devote their time and energy to the welfare of their family and the care of their home.

American society changed significantly again after World War II. Women left factory jobs they held during the war to get married and raise a family. Suburbs were built to house all of the returning veterans and their new families. Babies were born by the millions, schools were built, and suburban communities grew.

Another big change for modern society happened in the 1960s with the introduction of the birth control pill. Now, people could have sex without the fear of a pregnancy. This allowed for a freer attitude towards sex, both within and outside of the marriage.

Today's Marriage Challenges

Today, the average life expectancy in the United States is nearly 79 years. Women have full rights and opportunities, and marriage isn't the economic driver or social obligation that it once was. And yet, people are still getting married. Many of us look to marriage for emotional fulfillment, which can be a lot more complicated than the economic and parenting goals that were once the focus of a marriage.

Many modern couples are facing the reality of a 50-, 60-, or 70-year marriage. To achieve this, a marriage needs to be flexible, able to transform three or four times to survive and thrive over a lifetime. Partners must balance the security and stability of a marriage with independence and personal fulfillment. They must find ways to inject excitement and adventure into their life and their long-term relationship.

The challenge is to go through each transition of marriage gaining strength and skills as you move onto the next phase. Hopefully, you can find peace and harmony in your marriage, and transform it into something that is good for both of you over time. My parents did that, and they were still committed to each other seventy years after they said "I do."

To Marry or Not to Marry—That is THE Question

Before you were caught in the challenges of a long-term relationship—balancing kids, career, and a love life—there was a time when you made the decision to say "I do." Why did you choose to get married?

People get married for a variety of reasons. There are still strong social and religious pressures to get married, particularly for people who want to live together or have sex. Sometimes, people think that getting married is what should come next in their life, especially if they want to have kids. There are legal perks—tax deductions, immigration avenues, and healthcare benefits. And of course, there is the romantic notion of committing your life to the person that you love.

Indicators of a Happy Marriage

As marriage counselors and sex therapists, we have studied what makes people happy in their marriage. What are the signs that a couple is likely to be successful in their relationship together? What leads them to have marital and personal satisfaction? Here's what we've identified:

- **Shared values.** Having a common background is useful for the success of your marriage, because it often means that you share the same values. If you have a similar socio-economic, cultural, and religious background as your partner there are fewer differences to navigate. Being somewhat close in age can help you to understand each other as well.

  It's no surprise that traditionally, couples have been encouraged to marry people from similar families to their family-of-origin. Although interracial, cross-religious, and other "mixed" marriages can be successful, they often require additional skills to bridge gaps in values and cultural understanding.

- **Sexual chemistry.** Sexual attraction and chemistry are the single best prognostic tools in long-term marital satisfaction that we have seen. Couples who are sexually satisfied together are often calmer, kinder to each other, and better at solving problems together.

  While frequency of sex matters to many people, the quality of that physical connection is more important to most couples. A good sex life (or even just a "good enough" sex life) is the glue that keeps many couples bonded and together.

  Today's marriage should have an element of sexual compatibility and chemistry, or someone is likely to have an affair. Sexual chemistry is not something that is learned. It is either there or it is not. Attraction is often a matter of biology. More on that later.

- **Friendship.** We're often told to choose a spouse we can be good friends with. Choosing someone you like and get along with is important. You should have common interests and goals for your life together. It's also important to choose someone you are attracted to and who you can't keep your hands off of.

> **YUMMY Food for Thought:**
>
> Think about which of these qualities you and your spouse shared before getting married? Which do you still share today? Be specific. Which ones do you miss and why? Why were you attracted to your spouse?

Marital Satisfaction

To consider whether or not you're satisfied with your marriage, it's helpful to think about what you expect from your relationship. There are many different types of marriage today. They can be split into two broad categories:

- **Utilitarian** marriages have the more traditional goals of raising a family or advancing economically as the main focus. While that is good enough for some people, most people today want more out of their marriage than just child rearing and a beautiful home together.
- **Enriched** couples are connected in ways other than just raising their family and paying the bills. They sit down after the kids are in bed (if they have any children) to talk about their day and things of interest. They are couple-centered. They take vacations together, often without the children or pets, because they know that their marriage is sacred and needs time to grow and develop. They are connected and dedicated to each other in many ways.

Today, marriage can get a bad name, but the truth remains that married individuals are generally happier and healthier than their single, divorced, or widowed counterparts. Married couples, old and young, with and without children, repeatedly report higher levels of satisfaction with their lives overall.

Most couples today are looking for more from their marriage than just surviving. They seek the security that the institution of marriage can provide, plus some excitement and personal happiness. They want an enriched, YUMMY relationship. Enriched relationships survive and thrive because:

- The individuals involved take the time to understand their own thoughts and feelings.
- They communicate their wants and needs in a positive way.
- The couple is able to problem solve as issues arise and settle conflicts peacefully and respectfully.
- The couple spends time having fun, sharing interests, and celebrating their life together.

Despite the fulfillment marriage has to offer, many married people remain significantly unsatisfied in their relationship. Sometimes, the dissatisfaction is related to past traumas. In that case, personal self-healing can lead to a happier individual and a better relationship.

As I mentioned before, marital dissatisfaction is often related to the current stage in life and the stressors from that stage. Learning how to navigate the stages of a marriage and transform your relationship to fit your changing needs over a lifetime will help you succeed in staying happily married for a long time.

The Normal Stages of a Marriage

Knowing the marital life cycle can help you understand and process the normal ups and downs of a marriage. It's reassuring to know that some issues you are dealing with may just be a phase of life, not the signs of a flawed marriage or true incompatibility.

The Premarital Stage

Before a couple gets married, they usually feel a lot of attraction and excitement for each other. This is called the "honeymoon phase," despite the fact that it comes before the marriage. It is a natural high, a time when people fall in love with an idealized perception of their beloved.

Unfortunately, that idealized view of the partner is usually not completely realistic. As most people find out within a year, these dream images do not last forever. Marriages require effort. For some couples the honeymoon ends before the marriage even starts. Some people are torn about even getting married, getting cold feet before the big day.

Couples have to navigate the social, emotional, and financial stresses of wedding planning. Many are disappointed with something that happens on their wedding day, or during the highly anticipated wedding night. Maybe the expensive and exotic honeymoon trip doesn't go as planned. These can be the first real tests of a marriage.

Even so, most couples survive the wedding and honeymoon. During this pre-marriage time, it is useful to think through various wedding options, in order to prepare for success. Hint to pre-marital couples: Many couples plan a HUGE wedding event. Try to keep the financial obligations and the wedding weekend event schedule to a reasonable level. This hopefully will lessen unnecessary stress for everyone involved.

The Newlywed Stage

We often picture newlyweds in a state of bliss, but that isn't always the case. It's common for people to have a strong reaction to finally being married—some people feel trapped and suffocated, while others feel a sense of relief thinking that they're safe and secure, out of the dating scene for good.

While marital satisfaction is usually high at this stage, there is also a big adjustment to becoming a couple. There is a shift in priorities and previous relationships, as people pivot away from their childhood family and friends. They usually begin to focus on establishing a new nuclear family with their spouse.

During the newlywed stage, people must commit to a new system and a new way of life. Individuals need to change their roles and behaviors from daughter to wife; from son to husband. Spouses need to "cleave to each other" and begin to separate emotionally from parents, siblings, and friends.

For this to happen, couples should spend time alone together, instead of always being around friends, family, and co-workers. The rebalancing of priorities is an essential shift for most new couples. Couples need to invest time, money, and effort into their marriage.

The Early Years: Conception and Child Rearing

Couples who choose to become parents experience a big change in their marital roles. Having kids introduces many new responsibilities. The focus on the couple shifts as the family unit accepts new members into the system. Spouses are confronted with many changes in their life.

Sometimes, this happens even before a child is born. If a couple has difficulty conceiving, sex becomes a chore, losing all playfulness and pleasure. Couples who deal with infertility need to navigate the roller coaster of hormone treatments, doctors' appointments, and scheduled intercourse. These couples often deal with major disappointments and may blame each other for their challenges in getting pregnant.

The change in roles to parenthood is usually one of the most stressful times in a couple's life. Balancing time for individual needs, marital needs, and parenthood obligations can be overwhelming. This is a high-risk time for affairs for the husband, as he may feel left out with Mommy's attention being on the baby, young children, and her sleepless, achy body. Couples who have children with special needs, blended families, and adoptive families have additional stressors.

The stress of the early years of marriage explain why the "seven-year itch" is a common occurrence. Spouses (usually husbands) may be feeling left out and ignored after seven years of marriage, with two or more kids pulling on Mommy's apron strings and not yet in school. While feeling forgotten at home, the man may feel noticed and honored by other women at work and out in the big world. When that happens, trouble is just around the corner. As always, couples need to carve out special time to be alone as a couple enjoying some fun together, even during these busy years.

The Madonna-Whore Complex

Many men deal with a situation that is unconscious to them but has a powerful effect on their marital sex life. It is called the Madonna Complex or the Madonna-Whore Complex. It is an unconscious shift that happens for some men, depending on their religion and culture, when their wife transitions from being their lover, girlfriend, and hot sex partner to being the mother of their children.

Many men, especially of Catholic upbringing, put their wife up on a pedestal, seeing her as a blessed mother figure like the Virgin Mary (Madonna). What was once fun and kinky in the bedroom now becomes uncomfortable and unacceptable, because the wife is feeling maternal and the husband views her primarily as the mother of his children, no longer as his hot lover. Some men cannot get away from the thought, "That's the mouth that kisses my children."

In turn, the man needs a whore, some kind of lover or girlfriend, to fulfill those erotic sexual desires. Compartmentalizing the marriage from sex becomes a way of being a good father, in his mind, while satisfying his sexual needs.

Couples in this situation must realize what is happening, talk about it, and find playful ways to explore sexual needs that are satisfying for both partners.

Midlife Stage

After successfully coping with the stressors of early parenthood, the couple might expect relief when the kids start school. But in reality, parents still have 14 or more years where they spend time and energy raising school-aged children, teenagers, and possibly young adults.

The teen years are often stressful for the family system, as the young adults explore sex, drugs, and rock n' roll or—more likely these days—their phone addiction, gaming, and social media use. The couple must permit teens to move in and out of the family system as they prepare for adulthood and leaving their childhood home for good.

The focus of this period is often on career and financial obligations, including paying for college and preparing for retirement. This can be an emotionally trying time. Individuals are often split between the struggles with their teenagers and handling their aging parents, not to mention dealing with themselves.

In addition, people begin to face the reality of their own mortality as they navigate the deaths of good friends, family members, and co-workers. This is the time to plan for the final phases of their life as individuals and as a couple. This is the time to discuss any bucket list goals that have not been achieved yet, and make plans for them to happen.

The Empty Nest and The Golden Years

Some couples look forward to the day when their kids leave home and they are able to focus on each other. Others wonder how their marriage will flourish without the shared purpose of child rearing or how they will survive financially, especially if they have not prepared well. Many couples are not prepared emotionally or financially for retirement.

We talk about the empty nest, but this isn't always clearly defined. Many adult children return home after college, a failed relationship, or a health scare. These "boomerang" experiences may be a welcomed distraction if the couple is not well-connected, but they are problematic for most healthy couples who want the chance to be alone together during the final stages of their life together.

After the children leave home, there is usually a time of renegotiation of the marital system as the couple is now alone again. It is a time to begin relating to "the children" as adults, and to move into a retirement lifestyle.

While marital satisfaction commonly increases during this time, many couples also deal with physical, sexual, and emotional challenges or disabilities. This is a time for a re-evaluation of life: a midlife exploration of one's personal story—the accomplishments, relationships of all kinds, career successes and failures, and other significant events. It is a healthy and useful process. However, this exploration process can create a crisis if there have been many failures or if there has not been a good connection between spouses over their many years together.

Ideally, this is a time to reminisce about a YUMMY life together. Sadly, more and more couples today are getting divorced at this time because they did not stay connected throughout their marriage and now view their marriage as irreconcilable. They can afford to "start over" if desired, and many do. Today this is called a "grey divorce."

Negotiating Each Stage

While it is interesting to understand the typical goals and challenges of each stage of marriage, it is equally important for a couple to realize that they need to be able to define their own specific relationship tasks and goals, resolve their conflicts, and nurture their relationship in the process.

Successful negotiation of the relationship at each stage affects the transition to the next stage and the functioning of the marriage and family system throughout a lifetime. When couples do not deal with early challenges, they will probably face bigger obstacles later in life.

> **YUMMY Food for Thought:**
>
> What stage of marriage are you at now? What are your biggest stressors? How can you reduce those, and plan for the transition into the next stage? Which stages of marriage have been the most positive for you? Which have been the most challenging?

A Commitment to Marriage

Every year millions of brides and grooms make a vow to love each other "til death do us part." They say, "I do" and "I will." But approximately half of all marriages do not last until the death of their spouse. They end in a divorce.

While divorce may not be the end of the world, it is a stressful event that perhaps can be avoided if you have realistic expectations and the skills to deal with the situations that arise as you travel through a lifetime together.

I have long felt that couples should recommit on a regular basis. Many couples go through a rough patch and when they get to the other side, they make a decision to "stick it out." They have decided they "are in it for the long haul"—acknowledging that this kind of a commitment can be very powerful.

> **YUMMY Food for Thought:**
>
> Have you ever considered a divorce, why, what was going on? Have you and your spouse formally or informally recommitted to each other since your wedding day? Have you decided to stick it out and commit to each other for your lifetime?

Chapter 3

Love, Love, Love

MANY, MANY YEARS ago Israel was driving with our daughter, Amanda, listening to the oldies station on the radio when a song came on about "falling out of love." With the innocence and wisdom of a child, Amanda asked, "If you love someone, don't you always love them?"

Ah, the complications of love!

The 3 "L"s: Love, Lust, and Like

Love

So, what is love? The ancient Greeks had several words for love: *agape* (AH-gah-peh), *eros*, *philia*, and *storge*. *Agape* meant unconditional love; *eros* meant a passionate, sensual, and sexual desire; *philia* meant a brotherly love; and *storge* meant affection, like the love of your child.

When I talk about love in marriage, I am talking about *agape*—an unconditional caring for another human being. Agape is basic respect, the desire to see your partner be happy and healthy, and wanting the best for your good friend.

Almost everyone who comes to Marriage Quest has this basic love and caring for his or her partner. If they didn't, they wouldn't be doing this work with us. I often remind our couple that they obviously love each other. The question is do they *like* each other, and do they have enough *lust* for each other to make their marriage work.

Lust

Lust is that feeling of sexual attraction and desire. It's what most couples mean when they talk about "being in love." Israel and I call it having a "a juicy love life." While many people have been taught that lust is one of the deadly sins, we believe that lust is essential in a happy marriage if the couple wants a healthy long-term relationship that is committed and strong for a long time.

When lust and attraction are not in the marriage, there is a good chance that the husband or wife will find lust outside of the marriage. Affairs happen because the marriage is not exciting and alive with playfulness, attraction, desire, and sexy fun, as well as empathy and understanding.

Lust is the vital sign that we are looking for when we work with a couple. It usually is an indicator that this marriage can be rekindled and saved, regardless of how much the couple has disconnected—or for how long.

Like

Like means that you enjoy being together. You enjoy each other's company as friends and share some common interests and hobbies. You get along well and are a good team. Communication and problem-solving skills help couples to like each other more. Good communication helps each person feel appreciated, understood, and respected. This builds their connection on an emotional level. This couple is said to be well-bonded or attached.

Many couples are somehow calmer and happier when they are traveling together. Obviously, they are away from the stressors of home and work—

their "ordinary life." They behave like they are best friends and have more fun than they normally have when they are at home. They enjoy wining and dining and visiting the local attractions. Obviously, it is useful to be kind and "likable" at home too, not just on a vacation.

> **YUMMY Food for Thought:**
>
> Are the three L's present in your relationship now? Have there been times in the past when an element was missing? Does your partner see it differently?

Lucky in Love

We often talk with our couples about a triad that we call, The 3 L's: Love, Lust, and Like. In many situations in life "two out of three ain't bad". Marriage is a place where you need all three L's to be a strong and solid modern couple. Many couples survive on two of the three, but it seems clear that the happiest couples—the YUMMY couples—feel a bond from sharing their love, lust, and like with each other and for each other. These couples are what we call "lucky in love."

Fill Your Love Tank

Imagine your need to feel loved as a tank, like a gas tank. If life is good and you are feeling loved by friends and family, then your love tank is full. On the other hand, if you feel sad, hurt, and rejected often, then your love tank is probably empty.

People who feel disconnected from other humans often feel empty inside. They have empty love tanks, and they struggle on a regular basis to keep their tank full. They usually have a hard time feeling loved, even by the people who clearly love them. They are often prone to drug and alcohol use and abuse and other high-risk behaviors.

Filling the love tank can come from feeling more connected to other people. Saying hello to a stranger, volunteering, or even a good walk in nature can replenish your tank. In this fast-paced modern world, it is easy to feel disconnected, and it takes some effort to feel that loving connection again.

In a marriage, couples can strengthen their connection and bond by taking time to fill each other's love tanks. In order to do that effectively, you need to know what kind of fuel your partner prefers.

The Languages of Love

Pastor Gary Chapman developed a philosophy that explores five "love languages," the different ways that an individual may feel loved and show their love to other people. These languages can be used as a guideline to understand what is important to you and what is important to your spouse. They are great conversation starters.

Chapman's five love languages are:

- **Words of affirmation**: Praise, appreciation, encouragement
- **Quality time**: Showing all of your attention
- **Gifts**: Cards, flowers, jewelry, something that is "handmade," or money to buy something desired
- **Acts of service**: Such as helping around the house
- **Physical touch**: Including sexual and non-sexual touch; I think that sex can be a love language on its own for some people, different from the desire for cuddling, holding hands, and other forms of touch

Some therapists talk about consolidating the list into three love languages: words, touch, and behaviors. Maybe we can put everything into just two categories: words and behaviors. It is useful to determine what words you like and don't like and what behaviors you like and don't like.

However you look at it, it is very important to understand what makes you feel loved and what makes your spouse feel loved. How you feel loved and how your spouse feels loved can be very different. It often depends on what you learned growing up or your different values.

Over time I realized that when Israel bought me a pretty dress or beautiful jewelry, these gifts did not help me to feel loved and treasured. Sometimes I actually felt pressure to like the gift, even if I did not like it. Should I wear it if I don't feel good in it? Can I return it or exchange it? Sometimes it was more of a burden than a gift for me.

On the other hand, if he helps me with the dishes or washes my car—chores that take his time and energy—then I definitely feel loved, honored, and treasured. If he spends time truly listening and hearing what I am saying, then I am in marital heaven.

YUMMY Food for Thought:

- How do you show love to your spouse today?
- Do you know if your spouse values the ways that you show him or her love?
- How did you do it years ago?
- How do you know your spouse loves you today?
- Are there ways they showed you love before that you miss?
- How would you like them to show you more love today?

Remember, your love language may be a combination of all five languages. Labels don't matter, but it's important to be as specific as possible so you and your spouse can show love effectively to each other. Sometimes a specific word or behavior makes a big difference.

Being "In Love"

Being "in love" with your partner, spouse, or lover means having a combination of love, lust, and like. In other words, sharing a body, mind, and spiritual connection—a combination of a physical and an emotional attraction and bond. Some people describe it as an energized state of being, with hormones racing and raging.

We often hear women say things like, "My husband says that he loves me, but he is not 'in love' with me anymore." It is usually obvious that he loves her as a friend. He cares about her safety and well-being, but he does not feel attraction or lust anymore, if he ever did. They have drifted apart over the years and life has gotten in the way of them feeling close and connected. Fortunately, most couples can overcome these times of disconnection with some work if they had the chemistry before.

Often, not liking your partner is related to stress. If there was a good connection in the beginning of the relationship, it usually can be flipped around. Similarly, if there was lust and attraction at the beginning of your relationship, you can rediscover that excitement too. The attraction hormones (chemistry) are primal and usually can be reignited. With a little time and work, you can have the three L's back in your life.

On the other hand, it is difficult to rekindle something that never existed in the first place. Couples might have more trouble infusing lust into their relationship if it was never there. These are often couples who were good friends (not lovers) who fell into bed one drunken night, got pregnant, and "did the right thing" by getting married. Also, couples who lived together to save money on rent and then decided they might as well get married as the next relationship step. They, too, cannot kindle something that was never there or at least not very strong.

The Taste of Attraction

Attraction to another person happens consciously and unconsciously through all of your senses. You can be attracted to someone's beautiful eyes, luscious lips, strong-looking muscles, or large, perky breasts. You can like the sound of their voice, their sense of humor, or the smoothness of their skin. But two of the most significant factors in long-term attraction and sexual satisfaction specifically come through taste and smell.

The natural taste and smell of another person provide a hormonally-based experience related to their pheromones. I am not talking about deodorant, shampoo, or cologne. I am not talking about their sweaty body after a hard workout or their breath after a garlic-onion pizza. I am talking about the smell of another person's natural armpits, the nape of their neck, and the smell and taste of their sexual body fluids. That's their natural scent.

This can be a big issue for many couples who are really "just friends." They may enjoy spending time together, but when they think about the taste and smell of their partner, they may realize that they are not attracted to them in "that way." They are attracted to them like a brother or sister, but not as a lover.

Love Input and Output

The ability to feel loved by your spouse is connected to having felt loved as a child, just like the ability to trust someone has its roots in early childhood experiences. Everyone knows that a child needs to be loved by parents, grandparents, and other caretakers. What is not talked about much is that children need to have their love received by those people as well.

Consider a little three-year-old bringing a bouquet of dandelions to Mommy or Daddy. Some parents would say, "Yuck those are weeds!" while others might say, "Oh, thank you dear. They are beautiful!"

A child needs to have their acts of love received just as they need to feel loved. Love in affects love out. Luckily for those of you who did not have love-filled childhoods, you can change your story to reflect that you deserve to be loved and to be with someone who has the capacity to love you deeply.

When marriage is done right, you get to heal your childhood wounds through the marital relationship. So, work on your love life, your marriage, and yourself and see what is possible!

Chapter 4

Trouble in Paradise

EVEN SEEMINGLY HEALTHY families can have problems. There was a moment many years ago when I punched Israel in the mouth. I don't remember why or what we were talking about, but I was so angry that I lost control and punched him. I now take that event as an experience to remind me that even I ("Miss Calm") can lose control. From that incident, I learned the importance of calming down, self-soothing, sharing what I am thinking and feeling, or perhaps walking away so that I don't do or say things that I might regret.

Conflict Is Inevitable

All couples have conflicts and disagreements at one time or another. It is not the differences between spouses that are most important—it is how they negotiate their different desires.

It may be hard to believe, but a threatening situation can become an opportunity for growth and positive change. Many couples find that a well-resolved conflict actually brings them closer to each other. It builds trust, opens up lines of communication, and makes their marital bond even stronger than before.

However, in order to grow from conflict, you need to be able to handle the conflict in a healthy, productive manner. Just as physical pain can be a warning message that something is wrong with your body, difficulty in handling conflict and disagreements may be a warning sign that something needs to change in your marriage.

People tend to be passive or aggressive in dealing with conflict. They either avoid things and shut down or get loud and angry. They fight, flight, or freeze. Being assertive without being aggressive when you disagree is a skill worth learning and applying. It's also important to choose your battles carefully and wisely.

In other words: What is worth discussing? What is worth fighting for? What should simply be left alone? Sometimes OK is OK, and good enough is good enough.

The Marital Check-Up

The first question we ask participants when they sign up to do a Marriage Quest retreat with us is, "Why are you seeking a marriage (relationship) retreat at this time?" So, I ask you: ***Why did you pick up this book?***

- What is happening in your marriage?
- Or are you engaged to be married and afraid of having a bad marriage?
- Are you on the verge of a divorce looking to make the big decision?
- Or are you just looking for a few new tools for your toolbox?

This is where self-reflection is important. Grab a pen and journal, and think about the questions just mentioned as well as the ones below. Encourage your partner to do the same, if he or she is willing.

Hot Button Issues

What are the hottest issues? What topics are difficult to talk about? What do you fight about: Sex? Money? Cleaning responsibilities? The kids? Your nosy parents? Someone's infidelity (sexual or emotional)? Be specific. Is there any concern for your physical safety and well-being? Are you dealing with emotional stress and triggers from the past as well as today's events?

Change

How do you want to change to improve yourself and your marriage? How would you like your partner to change? How would you feel more loved by your spouse? Maybe you want them to listen better, spend more quality time, help around the house, have hot monkey sex with you, or have more romantic loving sex. Remember that change is the only constant in life. And yet, you have a say in what that change looks like.

Conflict

How do you deal with conflict with your spouse? How would you like to respond in an argument or disagreement with your spouse to get what you want in a positive way? How does your partner deal with conflict? How would you like them to deal with conflict with you?

Signs of Trouble

After you've done your marital checkup, it's time to assess your situation. Safety is always the first question in assessing any situation. According to the following criteria, do you have basic safety?

- **Sense of safety:** A safe home environment and neighborhood. Enough money to pay for your food, clothing, and shelter.
- **Physical abuse:** Anger and violence are what happen when people lose the ability to put into words what they are thinking

and feeling. Domestic violence usually occurs when one spouse is chasing the other one. If you are experiencing pushing, shoving, spitting, or throwing things, this is considered to be physical abuse in your marriage.

- **Mental abuse:** Verbal abuse, name-calling, and other manipulative or mean behaviors are unacceptable, too. Stonewalling, or shutting down without talking at all, cornering, baiting, or making threats (of divorce, suicide, or taking the children) are forms of mental abuse.

If you feel physically threatened or are being abused by your spouse, it is important to get help immediately. Don't confuse power struggles with abuse or, worse yet, convince yourself that violence is sexy. Many couples that we have worked with have had isolated experiences of some kind of abusive behavior. This is often during a time of high stress or after a traumatic event. Often, but not always, this is while they or their partner was under the influence of alcohol. Beware of drinking too much.

While physical and emotional abuse may happen during a stressful relationship time, people should be very concerned and seek help if it happens regularly. A marriage is in trouble if spouses are doing mean things to each other and if one or both spouses feels scared or unsafe. This is what I call, "Hitting below the belt." That includes:

- Physical or mental abuse, as listed above
- Yelling and screaming
- Name calling and belittling
- Lying about important matters
- Cheating (sexual or emotional affairs)
- Making ultimatums
- Shutting down and being unwilling to talk

There are other, less acute signs of trouble. If the list above is a red-light warning, the list below is a yellow-light warning. If these behaviors are happening in your marriage, it's time to slow down and take an honest look. If these behaviors continue over time, they can erode and ruin your marriage. By addressing them, you can turn a mediocre marriage into a YUMMY one.

- Increased silences or interrupting each other regularly
- Spending less time together, not having fun together, and feeling that life has become very serious
- Feeling fear, depressed, or anxious when going home
- Showing disrespect, blaming, and judging
- Increased drinking, drugging, gambling, or spending money
- Feeling defensive or "on the attack" all the time
- Spending less time on personal hygiene or cleaning the house
- Discussing divorce as the answer

Compatibility, Skill, and Ego

When couples come to us, we evaluate three things as part of the marital triage: compatibility, skill, and ego. As you perform your own evaluation, ask yourself and your partner these four questions:

- Are you truly compatible with each other or not? (see below)
- How strong are your relationship and communication skills?
- What challenges do each of you have regarding your individual "egos" or sensitivity and defensiveness?
- Would you feel jealous or relieved if your partner fell in love with someone else and lived happily ever after?

Compatibility

Many couples we work with believe that they are incompatible and that they should get divorced because of their irreconcilable differences. More often than not, however, these couples actually *are* compatible. They just need new communications skills and to learn how to handle their sensitive egos. Often, they have never been taught the skills of good communication and conflict-resolution, and they are being reactionary and hyper-sensitive with each other's words and body language.

True issues of incompatibility are things like:

- I want children and you do not
- I want to raise our children as Catholics; you want to raise them in the Jewish faith
- You want to make a lot of money and live in a fancy house; I don't want any of that
- You want to live in the countryside; I like the buzz of a big city
- I want to retire together and spend our golden years traveling and enjoying life; you want to work until they put you in a wooden box in the ground

Skills

We don't typically think of a marriage as something that requires specific skills, but of course it does. Emotional awareness, interpersonal skills, sexual intelligence, and good communication techniques are key to having a YUMMY marriage.

One of the most important skills in any intimate relationship is the ability to calm oneself down and de-escalate the situation. You both need the ability to self soothe, relax, stop the attacks, and either talk calmly or walk away. If each person can be responsible for their own behaviors, they will avoid defensive or aggressive reactions.

In return, communication will be fair and useful, and violence will be avoided. We often will joke that it is important to understand, "What is your shit, and what is my shit?"

Luckily, these relationship skills are very teachable and very learnable. Throughout this book you'll learn healthy, positive, and useful skills that can improve your marriage during stressful times and enhance your relationship in peaceful times. These skills are the building blocks to a good, strong marriage. Take them seriously and work on them. As we used to say, "Stronger marriages are not just a matter of chance!"

Ego

The term ego describes the opinion you have of yourself, your sense of self-esteem and self-importance, especially in contrast with other people. Obviously, how you see yourself in relation to other people can affect your relationships. When Israel and I talk about ego issues with our clients, we are talking about how a healthy ego or a weak ego affects the marital relationship.

A person with a weak ego (sometimes called a big or inflated ego) will often exhibit a sense of superiority and a judgmental attitude. This is an overcompensation for their insecurities. They are typically very sensitive, get defensive easily, overreact, take things personally that are not about them, or react quickly in their conversations. This creates a whole other layer of conflict and challenges in their closest relationships. Many people are very sensitive. Certainly, the couples that we work with are quite sensitive.

If both partners have weak egos and are sensitive, they will need to learn to calm down. This becomes their biggest challenge. Often two people who are both hyper-sensitive end up triggering each other. While it may seem counter intuitive, it is not their differences, but strangely their similarities, that become the problem. These similarities cause relationship blind spots and defensive reactions. We often recommend neurofeedback, biofeedback, meditation, or yoga (all of which can be done at home with guidance) to relax and de-escalate more easily and quickly.

Sources of Conflict

Close intimate relationships challenge many people because they replicate past experiences and feelings. As I said before, conflict is inevitable. In some ways it is predictable and in other ways it takes us by surprise. Understanding how, why, and when conflict may arise can help you better manage it within your relationship.

Past Experiences and Their Triggers

Intimate relationships can trigger old wounds. On our retreat we spend a lot of time with our couples shedding light on insights and understanding around their emotional triggers. We see that 90% of the issues that most couples deal with today have a basis in their past experiences. These are usually traumas or learned patterns from childhood or from other significant relationships in the past. Often, they stem from cultural and religious influences as well.

We all have pet-peeves or (in a more serious sense) triggers. The problems you face today are often upsetting because they feel similar to traumatic experiences that were upsetting in the past. Oftentimes, you're not actually upset about your relationship today. Instead, problems with your spouse cause the resurfacing of your own past wounds that you are working through consciously and unconsciously.

It's easy to point fingers at your spouse and blame them for what is wrong in your relationship or your life. Take a moment to notice that you have some responsibility for the situation as well. By looking at how you are part of the problem, you can work on healing yourself and becoming a better partner. Even small changes can make things better.

In order to change your relationship, you need to have honest insight into yourself. Learning who you are and how your past affects you today will help you to understand how you respond to various situations and people. Whether you like to admit it or not, your ethnic or cultural background, religious beliefs, childhood and young adult experiences, and perceptions of your parents' marriage or the institution of marriage in general all impact your relationships today.

> **YUMMY Food for Thought:**
>
> What are some ways that you get triggered? When is this likely to happen? What behaviors or words set you off? Do you know why these affect you so strongly? What are your partner's triggers and when are they most likely to appear?

Stress 101

Stress can have a huge impact on your marriage. When you're feeling stressed out you might revert to unhealthy methods of communication, snapping at your spouse, or disengaging from the relationship. Under stress, we often fall into the basic reactions of fight, flight, or freeze.

People feel stressed when their life seems out of control and they are pulled in too many directions. A single event may be manageable, but several stressful events or a crisis may leave you feeling totally overwhelmed. It is useful to get a reality check on the list of things that are stressing you out.

Stress builds over time and can leave you feeling exhausted and overwhelmed. Work, family, and financial pressure all contribute to stress, which could be eroding your marital relationship. Even positive events—like having a baby or starting a new job—can add to your stress level. This "positive experience" stress is called eustress.

> **YUMMY Food for Thought:**
>
> Make a list of things that are causing you stress or making you feel overwhelmed. You may find some relief and validation knowing that you are not being dramatic, but life has dished out one too many challenges. Next, determine what you can change and what "just is." Make a list of three things that you can work to change.

Crisis: Danger and Opportunity

Doing a marital check-up can be scary, because you might realize that your relationship is in a bad place. Many of the couples we work with are in a crisis situation, and you might be there too if you picked up this book.

It's important to remember that a crisis represents an opportunity for growth and change. The discovery of an affair can be a sign to some couples that things need to be different. It can be the beginning of a series of good changes, like spending more time together and making date nights a priority again, changing jobs, or perhaps moving the family to a new location.

At Marriage Quest, we often say, "If you look for the gift in the crisis, you will find it." So, try to look for the gifts—or at least a new opportunity. Try to see things from your spouse's perspective and focus on the bigger picture. Sometimes a crisis is a chance to save the marriage. That probably sounds strange and counterintuitive while you're going through it, but I know from experience that this is true.

Two Stages of Therapy

Unfortunately, in many cases psychotherapy has not helped our clients as much as I would hope for because of the focus on complaints, problems, and issues. I don't think that it is useful to talk about what is bothering you over and over again. It is essential to learn about what you want in life, what would make you happier, and how you can achieve those goals.

The first stage of therapy should be your opportunity to be witnessed by another human being. This is a time to tell your "sad and tragic tale." That is the traumatic story of your life: how you have been abused or neglected, how you are the victim, and how you've been wounded in many ways. It is a sad story. Unfortunately, many therapists get stuck in the telling and re-telling of their client's sad and tragic tale.

When therapy is done well the "sad and tragic tale" transforms into "a hero's or heroine's journey"—all of the struggles and traumas in your life have helped to make you who you are today. Some traumas have made you a stronger person, some have taught you that everything is going to be okay, you will be fine, and you'll do well even if whatever happened is not what you wanted at that time.

Fortunately, more and more therapists today are learning about positive psychology and the ability to help their clients see the opportunity in their crisis. So, tell your sad story, and be witnessed. Then learn how to grow and change, and perhaps even embrace your life's story.

Chapter 5

A Healthy Foundation

THERE HAVE BEEN times when Israel was mad and I thought that he is mad with me, but the truth is that he was frustrated with something totally unrelated to me—maybe his hay baler was not working, and the rains were coming in, or a bobcat ate our chickens. If I take it personally and respond in a defensive manner, then we have another layer of conflict. Obviously, that is not useful.

In the previous chapter we talked about your current relationship situation and how factors like stress and triggers of past experiences can contribute to conflict and resentment in your relationship today.

Now, let's learn how to respond in healthier ways when conflict arises. In the next chapter we'll delve into specific communication and problem-solving skills. Here, we're going to talk about an overview of patterns you need to recognize (and sometimes break) in order to communicate effectively.

Building Emotional Intelligence

We spend a lot of time with our retreat couples helping them to improve their "emotional intelligence." Gaining emotional intelligence means that you understand what you think and feel on the deepest level—and you know what you truly want.

Feelings are not good or bad, but they do impact a person's life and their relationships. It is very useful to realize that if you do not like what you are feeling, you can change what you are thinking. This in turn will affect your feelings.

Feelings

Most feelings can be placed into one of these six categories: anger, sadness, joy, excitement, fear, or shame. Each of the six feelings has many words that cover a range of intensity. If you're angry you might be "annoyed" or "enraged," for example. Understanding the six core emotions is helpful for healthy communication.

- **Anger** is actually a superficial feeling. It is designed as a defense mechanism to protect one's self. We say that it is like the tip of an iceberg: anger is what's above water, warning of deeper feelings beneath the surface such as fear, sadness, shame, hurt, or loneliness. Violence is the extreme manifestation of anger.
- **Sadness** can range from being somewhat down and unhappy to deep grief and sorrow. Suicide is the extreme manifestation.
- **Joy** is happiness, delight, peace-of-mind, and contentment. It's pleasure of many kinds, all the way to euphoria.
- **Excitement** can be positive or negative. Negative excitement is anxiety or anxiousness. Positive excitement is a thrilling sensation. Many people are excitement junkies looking for the next exhilarating experience, and therefore unable to enjoy their present moment.

- **Fear** is having a belief that someone or something is dangerous, likely to cause pain, or is a threat of some kind. This goes from apprehension and agitation to terror, panic, and trepidation.
- **Shame** is a deep emotion that defines oneself as being damaged goods, "a bad person." This should not be confused with guilt, which means "I have done something bad, but I am not a rotten apple." When someone feels guilty, they can make amends and fix the situation. A person who is full of shame cannot remedy the situation because they believe they are just a bad person. Shame is a very deep, painful, and damaging feeling.

Being able to name your feelings can help you to express yourself in a positive and useful manner. That's important, since bottling up feelings can leave you down and depressed or even lead to passive-aggressive behavior. The treatment for depression is healthy expression.

Confusion or frustration is a sign that you have multiple feelings happening simultaneously. Separating them out and exploring each feeling helps bring clarity and can make communication more manageable.

Dealing with Challenging Feelings

We teach a process that helps individuals deal with their challenging feelings. It is based on Rational Emotive Therapy (RET) and Rational Emotive Behavioral Therapy (REBT), developed by the Psychologist Albert Ellis.

The RET process is great in helping people challenge their negative beliefs and find healthier beliefs. It is good for turning feelings of rage, helplessness, or despair into calmer feelings. This is particularly useful in cases of infidelity or the sudden death of a loved one when feelings are usually quite painful and raw.

People can interpret the same situation in very different ways. Perception matters. Negative thinking (or "stinkin' thinkin'" as we call it) can create negative feelings. If you challenge your thoughts and beliefs, perhaps you can feel less stress, even without changing the situation at all.

It's tempting to think that events happen to us, and we react to them in a way dictated by the event. But the truth is there is not one correct reaction: how we think about the event leads to how we feel about it.

Consider two couples dealing with the aftermath of infidelity. One couple sees the affair as a wakeup call. They unite together to work on their marriage. The other couple ruminates on the betrayal and hurt, and ultimately divorces. It is not the event itself, but what they "told" themselves about the event that impacts how they respond.

Sensitivity, Overreaction, and Defensiveness

Defensiveness is the biggest problem in most intimate and close relationships. Hypersensitivity, defensiveness, and overreaction are at the root of the stress and conflict for many couples that Israel and I work with. As I mentioned before, this is actually a weak ego defense mechanism.

Sensitivity might not seem like a big deal, but it can lead to defensiveness and, in turn, an overreaction to situations. The issue arises when your sensitivity overwhelms you and dictates how you respond to your spouse in negative ways, usually making a "mountain out of a molehill."

Being hypersensitive happens when you take things personally that were not meant to be personal. Those situations can add fuel to the fire of any marital dispute.

Before you react personally to something that your spouse says or does, try to get to the root of what has actually upset him or her and show some empathy and understanding. This will help you move forward with a productive conversation and an exploration of possible solutions. Hopefully your spouse understands why they are getting triggered and what they need. Unfortunately, they may be blind to any insights at that moment.

Maybe you are part of the problem, but maybe your spouse just needs to vent about a letter from the IRS or the fact that something valuable fell and broke. By better understanding and managing your own ego, hypersensitivity, and defensiveness, you'll have a more peaceful relationship. It is very important that individuals learn to calm down, "chillax," and not take things so seriously and so personally. When you're both doing this, the marriage will benefit. This is called teamwork.

From Passive and Aggressive to Assertive

Here is a continuum line to show a range of human behavior and personality types. The communication skills that we teach in our retreats and are presented in this book are basically about being an assertive person, also known as "Assertiveness Training 101."

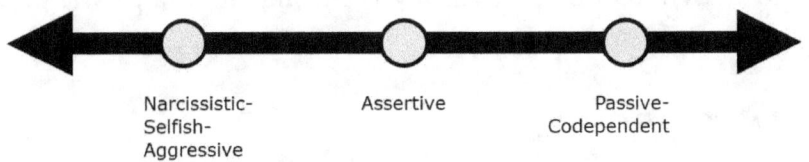

Narcissistic-
Selfish-
Aggressive

Assertive

Passive-
Codependent

On one end of the continuum is the person commonly referred to as "Type-A." This person is aggressive, selfish, and driven. Some people describe them as being narcissistic. On the other end of this continuum is the person who is passive and subservient. Some people call them codependent or "other-centered."

No one is passive or aggressive 100 percent of the time, but problems occur when someone is predominantly aggressive or predominantly passive. People tend to be passive or aggressive by nature, and in many marriages one person tends to be aggressive and the other tends to be passive.

Aggressive People

People who are on the aggressive side are usually mean. They're focused on themselves, rather than on another person's well-being. They tend to be intense, angry, pushy, and demanding. They can be aggressive physically and verbally, anywhere from being physically abusive, to name-calling, to making belittling statements, or giving angry looks. To a sensitive person, statements like, "You should___" or "Why didn't you___?" may sound mean and controlling. Aggressive people often get their way, but other people typically don't want to be around them.

Passive People

People who are passive tend to be the caretakers of the world. They are nice, friendly, happy to help out, and usually focused on other people more than themselves. Unfortunately, passive people (often women) are so focused on their spouse and children that they do not know what their body and soul needs. In the worst-case scenario, they may become sick and have no awareness of those needs. Everyone might like a passive person, but they rarely get their needs met.

Passive-aggressive

To complicate things, some people who are generally passive can be passive-aggressive at times. They might be late often, forget to pick up the dry-cleaning, break a favorite object "by mistake," make a sarcastic remark, or forget a special day or event. Often when the passive person "gets their voice" the pendulum swings from being passive to being aggressive. I call this newfound aggressive state: push-back or the FU mode.

Assertiveness

The healthiest behavior tends to be in the middle of this continuum, between passive and aggressive. This is called being assertive or pro-active: asking for what you want, without being forceful or pushy. Assertive people usually get their way *and* usually get along with others. Yet sometimes, especially when someone is learning to be assertive, other people may feel bullied, hurt, or rejected. Still, learning to be assertive can be useful and can benefit your marriage greatly.

When Selfishness is Good

Being assertive is a healthy form of selfishness. For many passive people, it seems wrong to "stand up" and speak for themselves. Many women (and some men) who were raised with strong religious beliefs find it challenging to share what they want from other people. They believe that they are supposed to take care of others even at the expense of their own well-being. It's the old airplane analogy: when the oxygen masks drop, you need to apply your own before helping others.

Everyone is entitled to their opinion and should be able to ask for what they want or need. They may not get it, but they have the right to ask for it. Everyone should have a voice and be able to speak their mind in a kind and loving way. Keeping it positive is the key.

We all need to be assertive in asking for what we need. Most people need some personal time without their children or their spouse. Maybe for you it's a bubble bath, or a yoga or art class, time in the woodshop, or exercise time. Remember, taking healthy quality time for yourself will benefit you, your marriage, and your children in the long run.

Stress Management and Cooling Off

There's little we can do to stop the stressful events that life throws our way. Even positive change can be stressful. However, we can change how we respond to life's events. Your ability to better cope with "life" will help you and your family. Most people deal with challenging situations with a stress response: fight, flight, or freeze. Like an animal being stalked by a predator, humans respond in an instinctive manner by running away, fighting back (verbally or physically), or shutting down (freezing).

These are survival techniques and are useful as a first line of defense, but they can become harmful when they're overused. If you are in a war zone, it's beneficial to be on high alert, but if you're in a safe location a constant stress response can be damaging to your well-being. You must learn to manage your life before the stress begins affecting your health.

How to Calm Down and Rebalance

Many of our couples need to wait a month or two after contacting us until we can meet with them to work on their relationship. Therefore, I often make suggestions on things that they can do to calm down and relax in the meantime to make the best of their waiting period.

These are some of the techniques that I suggest:

- **Breathe:** learn how to take some calming breaths, meditate, or give yoga a try; even a few deep breaths a day can make a big difference
- **Get Physical:** exercise, dance, or have sex with your partner to get your blood flowing and create some happy hormones
- **Get Creative:** journal, draw, write, play an instrument, or sing
- **Get Outside:** spend time in nature, go for a walk, work in the garden, spend time by a body of water if possible
- **Have Fun:** visit a museum, read a new book, or go to a show; hang out with a friend doing healthy activities
- **Change your diet:** make it more nutritious or try some new recipes
- **Sleep more and nap:** extra sleep or a midday nap can help you feel better able to handle stress; cuddle with your lover, your child, or your pet

Is Change Possible?

Many therapists tell their clients, "You cannot change your spouse. You cannot change anyone except for yourself." I disagree. Spouses change each other. They influence each other, and have an impact on each other. Therefore, they change each other. We've seen many times that a spouse's effort to be kinder, smile more, and listen with an open heart and mind has led to a positive response and positive changes in their spouse.

Sometimes change is slow, but other times it happens instantly. Most people agree that everything changes in a moment when something bad happens, like a car accident or an unexpected death.

The opposite is true too: positive change can also happen instantly. Change happens in the moment when a couple really sees that they are still "in love" with each other. They have both been pig-headed, stubborn, and mean to each other for such a long time, but in a moment of realization, we see couples fall back in love. It happens all of the time here. We call it a miracle, and miracles do happen.

So, how can you make changes in your relationship? The formula that we use for help in making change is:

Understanding + Action = Change

Understanding is the ability to truly know who you are, how your past has influenced you, why you get triggered, what you want from your spouse to heal, as well as why you were attracted to your spouse, and what you want from them in the future. It also means trying to understand your partner: What are they trying to say? What do they want from you or anyone else?

Action is learning how to ask for the things that you desire in a kind and loving manner. Learning to keep your anger and frustration in line is useful for this step. If you're calm, you'll be wise in your choice of words, tone, and body language. Keep it positive. A calm tone and facial expression can be very useful.

My story of taking action is: I understand that it is important for me to feel like I have some financial control in my marriage. Sometimes I want to buy something for myself or pay for something for one of our children or grandchildren. Israel might not agree with my plan, so I might need to negotiate the idea. Usually, I do not want to discuss or defend my choices or make some kind of deal. I like the excitement of buying something for myself or giving money to support a dream of a family member.

So, I took action to change this situation. I set up two new bank accounts. One for Israel and one for myself so that I could spend some of my money without needing to discuss, explore, or defend my decisions. By understanding Israel and myself and taking action, I was able to make a positive change in our relationship.

Other times, change is as simple as breaking bad habits. You'd be surprised at how many of the issues that couples deal with that can be corrected by adjusting their patterns and habits. Adjusting your habits can happen fairly easy. It takes a month or two but with a conscious effort many bad habits can be changed.

Another story is: When our children were pre-adolescent, it was a very busy and stressful time for both Israel and me. We were renovating our home, raising the kids, working long hours, and navigating tight finances. Israel was very stressed, so I asked him if there was anything I could do to help him with his stress level. He suggested that if the kitchen was cleaned up by 3 p.m. then he would be able to prepare dinner without the kitchen mess—that would make him a lot happier. This was a habit that I could easily change, and it made a big difference in our stress level and marital satisfaction during that time.

Change is possible, but you must figure out which things you can change, and which are out of your control. Don't waste your time dealing with situations that probably cannot be changed. Sometimes you cannot change other people or the situation that you are in. Sometimes you can. Know the difference!

Transition Times

What have been the most stressful times in your marriage? For most people events such as moving, changing jobs, or having a baby are among the top of the list. Often those events between the old familiar and new unknown are hugely stressful.

Similarly, daily transitions are often a time of conflict for couples (or for parents and children). Many couples have a blow up just before bedtime, or argue when one spouse is leaving for the day or arriving home after work.

These transition times are a great place to change how you interact with your spouse. By being mindfully positive with your partner, you can change a stressful situation into a new connection, even if you only give a 30 second hug or a big smile.

> **YUMMY Challenge:**
>
> Challenge yourself to take two minutes a day to be kinder and more positive. By dedicating 30 seconds to connect at these key transition points, you can begin to change your relationship for the better.
>
> - When you get up in the morning
> - When one person leaves the house
> - When the second spouse returns home
> - When you go to bed together, or when the first person is ready for bed
>
> Focus on positivity and kindness for these two minutes each day, and see how quickly change happens!

Chapter 6

Communication 101

HEALTHY COMMUNICATION IS essential in a deeply connected marriage. No matter what the issues are between spouses, their ability to communicate well together can make everything a lot better. At the same time, a lack of good, healthy communication skills will make everything a lot worse.

Because of that, working to improve your relationship skills and techniques is always highly beneficial. Improving your communication and problem-solving abilities and keeping the conversation positive and productive is the cornerstone of our work in our retreats and here, in this book. We will give you the tools to communicate in a positive way, even when you're stressed or emotional. Sometimes simply saying, "please" or "thank you" can make a BIG difference; so can listening without asking a bunch of questions.

At its core, good communication is simple: One person shares what they are thinking and feeling in a positive and useful manner. The other person listens with interest and patience.

Unfortunately, it's much harder in practice than it sounds. When couples are under stress their communication often becomes negative and destructive. Defensiveness and negative reactions create conflict in most relationships. Empathy and love help to smooth out tension and create pathways to a better connection. Even small changes, like speaking with a respectful tone of voice and keeping open and receptive body language can change your experience.

A note: The skill-building techniques we teach to every couple is based on a training process called Relationship Enhancement (RE)—not to be confused with Rational Emotive Therapy (RET), which we covered in the previous chapter. RE is one of the best relationship enrichment skills programs available.

Mastering the Positive Spin

A healthy, productive conversation is pro-active, focused, and calm. Consider this story: Years ago, my mother took a long road trip with a friend and his girlfriend. They were driving down a winding road when the man's girlfriend asked him to slow down. She said, "I'm scared; my hands are like ice." He slowed down immediately with no negative response.

In the car, my mother remembered being a child with her father driving fast and her mother shouting "Are you trying to kill us?" She noticed how the girlfriend's calm tone and positive statement got such a good reaction. The girl had expressed her personal feelings and asked for what she wanted rather than accusing him, making him feel defensive, and starting an argument.

If the girlfriend had complained about his reckless and inconsiderate behavior in a judgmental manner, she probably would have gotten a defensive response. Talking about yourself and how you can feel better is key. Calm and polite words work much better than judgments and complaints, and they are usually positively reinforcing.

One of the most profound things we teach couples to do is to put the "positive spin" on whatever they are trying to say. In other words: to "accentuate the positive and eliminate the negative." Share what you want, need, or desire instead of complaining about the things that you do not like or your partner's shortcomings. Behavioral science teaches us that you get whatever you focus on, so focus on what you want, like, and need.

With this simple but challenging change, your communication will improve. Your spouse is more likely to listen to what you're saying, rather than getting defensive; you are more likely to get what you want; and you will avoid a power struggle.

After many years of marriage research, Dr. John Gottman and the Gottman Institute in Seattle came to a profound conclusion: couples should have at least a 5:1 ratio of being positive to being negative. That means you should use five times the amount of kind words and positive body language as you do angry, critical words, or harsh body language. Gottman says that kindness and generosity are the most important qualities in a successful marriage.

Learning how to communicate positively can have a huge impact on your marriage. Negativity and pessimism can ruin even the best of relationships. The power of positive thinking and the use of kind words are critical, not just in marriage but in all relationships. Kindness matters. Learning how to communicate positively is a great tool toward improving your marriage and your personal happiness.

Simple Changes for Better Communication

Adopting a positive spin is Step One for better communication. However, there are also other specific steps that you can take as well. Making small changes to the way you speak with your partner can be a catalyst for change. Here are four steps you can implement today.

1. Put your negative thoughts in the past tense

When talking with your spouse, put negative behaviors in the past tense if possible. Then, put positive and hopeful ideas in the present or future tense. For example, "I didn't like it when you came home late without calling or texting. I am really excited to think that you will give a quick call when you know you will be late. That would help me to feel more loved and respected." This shows that you're willing to leave behind negativity and work toward a more positive future.

2. Recognize trigger words

Just like many of us have behavioral triggers, we often have words that trigger us as well. These words start a negative spiral because of the emotions they tap into. Knowing your own trigger words and those of your partner can help you communicate more peacefully, and without unintentionally stepping into a minefield.

For example, If Israel starts a sentence with phrases like "You should_____" or "You know, Cathie_____" I can get instantly annoyed and defensive, because I experience it as a demand. He's wise to avoid those words, and we get along better when he does.

3. Play with the power of 'yes'

How you respond to a comment from your partner can set the stage for how the conversation will move forward or spiral down to a bad place. So, respond in a positive manner. When your partner expresses an opinion or has a request it can be useful to respond by saying "yes" instead of "no." In addition, say "and" instead of "but."

For example: If Israel asks me if I am ready to go to dinner and I'm not quite ready I might say, "No, I'm not ready." It is better for him if I say something like "Yes, I should be ready soon, and not quite yet."

When you make these changes in how you respond, you validate what your partner has said. This makes them feel understood and lays a positive groundwork for the rest of the day.

4. Use please and thank you

When you were young you were probably taught that please and thank-you were magic words. I was so enamored with them that I used to count the times I said or received them each day. It may sound silly, but I think it was a useful intention. People enjoy those words and experience them as acts of kindness, love, and respect. Therefore, they magically open the door to a positive connection.

In addition to the basic manners of please and thank you, substituting "thank-you" rather than "I'm sorry" can be empowering. Saying thanks is a form of gratitude and is positive, while apologies are often quite negative and self-deprecating. Instead of saying, "I'm sorry I did not do the dishes yet." Try saying, "Thank you for your patience while I finish my project. I should be able to get to the dishes in about an hour."

> **YUMMY Food for Thought:**
>
> Take time to think about your own trigger words. What are some of them? Do you know why they affect you? Do you have certain memories tied to these words? After your own reflection, consider discussing this with your partner.

Planning for a Productive Conversation

When it comes to communicating effectively, the skills start before you even open your mouth. We teach our couples to structure the conversation for success before they begin speaking. Here's what that involves:

Timing

Timing is critical, especially for emotional, contentious, or just important conversations. This is especially true if one or both partners are very sensitive people.

Don't begin a conversation when your spouse is busy or too tired. Instead, choose a time when they can hear what you are trying to say and not react defensively. Never have a serious conversation when one of you has had more than a drink or two. Alcohol can fuel the conflict.

Bring up a challenging conversation when you have enough time to discuss the issue fully or at least give it a good beginning. Some topics require several conversations, not just one, so do not rush the conversation. Allow it the time and space that it needs and deserves.

Sometimes it seems like there is never an ideal time to talk, but don't use that as an excuse to avoid important conversations. I used to think there was no good time to talk with Israel about something negative. If he was in a good mood, I didn't want to ruin that, and if he was in a bad mood, I risked making it worse. Timing is very important, but sometimes you just have to dive in and begin the conversation.

Introductory Statements

It is very useful to use an introductory or preface statement when checking to see if someone is available to talk, or when you are bringing up a challenging subject. Israel calls it "meta-communication." I call this "testing the waters." You can use basic introductory statements like:

- "I want to talk with you about something. Is this a good time?"
- "This is really important to me."
- "When would be a good time to talk in the next day or two?"

Conversation Location

It is usually best to have big conversations in-person—not via phone, email, or text. Some people introduce the idea of having an important conversation or the specific topic while not in-person, but it is best to process the information together.

Begin your conversation somewhere that you both feel safe, where you can be uninterrupted, and you're on equal footing. Israel and I used to sit on the sofa or in our big bathtub after the kids went to bed. We shared a glass of wine, water, or a cup of tea.

If you are concerned for your safety, choose a public space. Otherwise, a calm private location is better than a busy restaurant or bar. Some couples have their best talks while driving. I do not recommend this. Stressful conversations can be as distracting and as dangerous as is texting while driving. Plus, one person may feel trapped in the vehicle and respond angrily, like a caged animal.

Don't have intense conversations in your bed. Save your bed for sex, sleep, cuddling, and sweet pillow talk, not for heavy conversations. In fact, we recommend to our couples on retreat here that they get out of bed and move to the sitting area of their hotel if they need to talk about their feelings that are in the way of being close and intimate together. That way you can deal with the issue outside of the bed, and your conversation won't be the elephant in the room next time you want to be intimate.

Plan to Speak Positively

Take time to consider what you want to talk about before you get started. What do you want and how can you convey that in a positive and focused way? Remember the positive spin and to focus on you, not your partner.

Most people naturally go to a negative place in their communication. It's easier to share what we don't like, instead of what we want or need. And yet, blaming your spouse and sharing anger and frustration will not have a good outcome. Take some time to understand what you really want and flip your problem into a more positive, healthy, and useful statement.

Before your conversation, ask yourself:

- What do you want?
- What would make you feel happier?
- What would make you feel safer or more loved?
- What would make you feel closer to your spouse or more attracted to them?

Figuring that out can take some time, so it might be helpful if you both know the conversation is coming. That way, you can journal or reflect ahead of time and come into the conversation with focused, positive talking points. Hopefully, that leads to a good outcome for both of you.

Being a Good Listener

If no one is really listening, then communication will probably break down very quickly. Most of us have been taught how to speak, but we're rarely taught to listen. And yet, being a good listener is an important skill to learn. To be a good listener, you need to slow down and pay attention to the person speaking.

Most people listen with the intention of responding. It's much more useful to listen with the goal of truly hearing what is being said to you. You need to focus on the person speaking. Stop thinking about how you are going to respond to what is being said, and how you can defend your position.

Active Listening

In our communication work we teach a skill-building process called active listening. For most people it feels annoying and cumbersome at first, but the results are often quite amazing. When spouses actually listen to each other, change can happen, even in a moment. We see this kind of miracle all of the time.

During active listening, the person who is listening mirrors back to the speaker what they have said. The listener acts like a parrot, using the speaker's words, and emphasizing what they are emphasizing. This is not a time to interpret or add your own thoughts, and yet be careful to avoid sounding sarcastic. Listen lovingly and *truly hear* what is being said. Use the speaker's exact words if possible. Using the speaker's words can be very powerful. Some people are really connected to their chosen words.

Mirroring back does not mean that you agree with what is being said.

It also does not mean that you necessarily even understand what is being said. It is a sign of respect, love, and compassion. It conveys the message that, "I care enough about you to listen patiently, and to help you to clarify what you think, what you feel, and what you really want."

The principles of active listening can be replicated at home by mirroring some of what your partner says. Be attentive and show that you are interested. Look at your spouse whenever possible. Signal that you care about them and that you want to hear what is being said. Be honest if you are losing patience and need to respond, or if you need to take a break from the conversation for any reason at all. It's okay if you need them to repeat what they just said because you drifted off (for any reason). Just tell them.

People often repeat themselves when they do not feel heard. Mirroring back to your partner might stop them from this repetition. If they keep repeating, try showing some emphasis when you mirror back, such as, "You *really* want me to know____" or "It is *very* important to you that I____"

Consider this example of an active listening conversation:

- **Spouse 1:** "I'd feel closer to you if you would snuggle with me on the sofa when we watch TV. I really like that feeling of connection with you."
- **Spouse 2:** "You'd feel closer to me if I would snuggle with you on the sofa when we watch TV. You really like that feeling of connection with me."

If the statement is more than a sentence or two obviously it needs to be paraphrased. Try to catch the important words, such as feeling words like happy, sad, angry, or scared. "You're really happy about that!" or "That scares you." Active listening may feel awkward at first, since it is a different way of talking. It's like learning a new language. It feels uncomfortable to speak French or Japanese the first times you try it, so be patient with yourself and with your partner.

Empathy

Empathy is the ability to understand someone else's feelings, to see things from their eyes, or to "walk a mile in their moccasins."

This is what therapists tend to do and what many girlfriends do together naturally. Typically, more men need work in this department than women, but plenty of women need help here too.

There are many times when I have wanted to explain to Israel why his brother or sister said or did something. Israel, however, needed me to show him understanding for what he was feeling, not to explain or defend anyone else. Explaining someone else's position was not useful to him at that moment. By showing empathy for his feelings, I avoided conflict. After showing understanding I can then explain what someone else meant.

Listen to what your spouse is saying as well as to what they are not saying directly. For example, when someone says, "When will you be home?" It's likely they want to spend time together, and not because they want to micromanage your schedule.

By listening with empathy, you can understand where your spouse is coming from. If you understand their motivation, you'll be less likely to become defensive and react negatively. This is a great way for spouses to develop feelings of trust and feelings of greater safety and security. It really pays off.

Fix-it Mode

Many men and some women are very good at problem solving and fixing things. When their spouse presents a problem, they have an urge to immediately present a list of solutions.

Yet, when it comes to relationships, most people want to be heard first. They want a chance to express their concerns and emotions before suggestions for solutions are made. Timing is important here.

As the daughter of an engineer, I love detecting and fixing problems, but there have been many times when Israel requested that I "just listen" and mirror back first. I can offer any suggestions afterwards. Sometimes understanding the problem and offering compassion are more useful than offering suggestions of how to fix it. This type of coaching may lead to your spouse fixing their problem on their own or self-correcting.

How to Speak

As the speaker, there are a number of things you can do to help the conversation stay positive and productive. These suggestions are particularly important during stressful times.

Stay Focused and Brief

Stick to one subject at a time. Don't bring up the last ten years of issues. Keep it short and sweet. Long, drawn out conversations usually end up in a bad place, so take the most important issue or goals and get to the point quickly. Share the theme of your issues, or give the Cliff Notes version.

Use "I Statements"

A good "I statement" communicates what you think, what you feel, and especially what you want. The intention of the statement should be positive and useful, not to blame or judge your partner.

To make a more productive statement, focus on what you want—the outcome that you hope to achieve. Consider how these different "I statements," which address the same issue, would be received:

- I find you very rude when you interrupt my calls.
- I hate it when you interrupt me when I am on the phone.
- I would like it if you would wait until I'm off the phone to speak with me. I feel respected and calm when I have space to finish my conversations. They are really important to me.

All of these are "I statements," but the first is blaming. The second one is focused on the problem, not the solution. The third statement is likely to lead to a more respectful and calm conversation.

Focus on Desired Feelings

When you are discussing problems, focus on your feelings, especially how you would like to feel. Try using this framework:

- I feel _____ when you _____.
- I would feel _____ if you _____.

The first allows you to address a problem using an "I statement." The second allows you to present a solution using an "I statement." It allows you to express what you want and need in a positive and useful way.

Consider these different statements:

- "I am so angry because you interrupted me on the phone."
- "I would feel happier and closer to you if you waited until my call is finished to talk to me."
- "I would love it if you would just slip me a note when I am on the phone so I know that you want to talk."

All of these allow you to express your feelings. However, the first is likely to provoke a defensive response. The second and third allow you to express your feelings and share what you want and need without causing a defensive response.

Eliminate Questions

Questions might seem harmless, but they can be a sneaky way of trying to get information from someone else without sharing yourself. Questions are what attorneys use to trap people. They can be manipulative.

Early in a relationship questions are a fun way to learn about your date. Fast forward twenty years, three kids later, maybe an affair or two, and now even simple questions like "what time is it?" or "what do you want for dinner tonight?" can lead to an argument.

So, to avoid these land mines, we tell couples to **avoid all questions** when there is stress in their relationship. We ask our couples on retreat to talk with each other without asking any questions for a period of time.

Questions aren't inherently bad and can be useful at times. But when an intimate relationship is strained, most questions elicit a defensive response and make everything a lot worse. They create a punitive atmosphere.

When you have a question that you want to ask your spouse, instead ask yourself what is behind the question. What am I thinking? What am

I feeling? What do I want? What do I need? Then ante up and share what you want and need instead of asking the question.

Behind most questions is a more honest and direct statement. Work on understanding what it is, and then deal with the awkward feelings around asking for what you want. While it will feel strange at first, it is better in the long run for both of you.

Consider this example: if you are sitting at a restaurant, looking at the menu the typical question is, "What are you thinking of getting?" Think to yourself, why are you asking this question? Do you want to know the appropriate price range, or are you interested in sharing two dishes? Instead make a statement, like, "If you get the sirloin steak and I get the fish and chips, I can get some steak and some fish."

Don't Make Demands or Commands

Demands and commands make people feel defensive and angry. After all, no one likes to be told what to do. If you need to make a request of your partner, be sure to say please and thank-you. Those simple words make a world of difference.

Of course, marital roles matter here, as does the setting. For example, if I'm building something with Israel and he's in charge of the project, I don't mind if he says, "Get me the hammer and nails." In that moment, I am his helper and I'm comfortable with being told what to do. Yet, if I am running around doing my chores and he says, "Get me a glass of water" I might get annoyed.

Don't Leave Room for Assumptions

When we don't know what someone else is thinking, human nature is to fill in the blanks with negative thoughts. Because of this, it is better to share something that may seem less than ideal, instead of leaving it up to your partner's imagination.

For example, consider that you don't want to kiss your spouse because they have bad breath. If you simply turn away when they try to kiss you, they might assume you do not love them. Instead of risking that false assumption, it's better to have an awkward conversation where you ask your partner to brush their teeth or use a breath mint.

This goes both ways. The speaker needs to be clear about what they want, and the listener needs to not assume. If you have an assumption about your spouse, check it out. We call it "getting a reality check."

Go Deeper

Quite often couples argue about surface issues. Many couples don't even remember what they were arguing about. Try to figure out what is really going on for you and share those deeper wants and desires.

Are you really arguing about the dishes, or is the issue that you believe you're carrying the burden of the household chores? Perhaps you feel lonely or ignored. Often people are sad, lonely, scared or disappointed, but rather than addressing those feelings or concerns, they focus on surface issues, like garbage not being taken out or dishes piling up in the sink. Go deeper. What is really bothering you? What do you want? Share your desires in a constructive way.

Moving Through Conversation

Now that we've covered how to be a good listener and how to speak in a positive, focused manner, let's consider how to structure your conversation. Having a framework means that both spouses have the space they need to communicate their thoughts and feelings and truly feel heard.

Take Turns Speaking and Listening

Your conversation should have two roles: speaker and listener. It is important to take turns in each role. The speaker should have the floor for two to four rounds (as speaker and listener; speaker and listener). If you try to switch back and forth too often it will get confusing. If the speaker is finished, they can say, "I'm done. You can have the floor."

If the listener is getting antsy or having a difficult time listening and needs to speak, they can request the floor. Taking care not to interrupt, say something like "I can mirror back to you what you just said, and then I want to respond to what you're saying. I'd like to speak." If your heart is pounding, you probably need to speak. Ask for "the floor."

Like I said, questions are usually antagonistic or manipulative, but they can be used when talking about the process of your communication. It's okay to say, "Are you done?" or "Did I get that right?" or "Can I talk now?"

Taking Time Out

It's only helpful to have a conversation as long as you are both staying positive, focused, and productive. Sometimes couples need to take a break from talking because one or both people are angry or even just tired from a long day. Be smart and realize when this is happening.

If both of you *need* to speak, then no one is probably listening well. That is a good time to take a break. If you call for a "time out" be sure to schedule a time to pick up the discussion again. That way the person trying to talk feels respected and loved, not blown off, rejected, minimized, or dismissed.

It is important to stay calm during discussions. Some conversations cannot be cleaned up in a short time frame. Some conversations need extra time, and calling a time out is not a failure. While it's useful to go to bed feeling calm, and not feeling angry, sometimes it is better to take a break than to push for closure before bedtime.

Don't Push or Escalate

Violence can happen when people can't put into words what they are thinking and feeling. Violence and the lack of impulse control may happen when one person does not want to talk and the other person is chasing them demanding to talk *now*.

In this situation someone usually gets hurt physically or emotionally. If you find your conversation shifting this way, moving away from the set structure of speaker and listener, stop. Suggest a period of time to cool down. If the tension is very high set a time to get together in the near future to continue the discussion again. Tabling the discussion can be very wise when anyone is angry and reactive.

When it comes to having productive conversations with your spouse, remember:

> **Set your sights on a good direction.**
> **Look for a positive relationship outcome.**
> **Don't bring something up just to dump it**
> **or get it off your chest.**
> **Work to repair your relationship after a conflict.**

Check-in Conversations

We suggest that couples have a planned "check-in" with each other every day while they are trying to flip their marriage around into a better place. This isn't a major conversation about tough topics, it's a quick gauge of progress. More importantly, it is a time to practice the communication skills described above in their pure form.

Daily check-ins should be between five and twenty minutes long. There is no excuse for not being able to find five minutes together. On the flip side, it is a discipline to be able to "put your swords down" and stop the conversation after 20 minutes, even if it is deep and perhaps conflictual. Many couples use a timer of some kind to tell them when the 20 minutes is up.

Ideally, couples should schedule their check-in for the same time each day. This creates a daily habit, and the conversation is more likely to happen if it is in the schedule. Obviously, there will be times when it needs to be rescheduled, but it should not be skipped.

The check-ins should follow the rules of good communication and active listening described earlier. Share your thoughts and feelings with a positive focus, mirror back, and take turns being speaker and listener.

Put your negative opinions into past tense. The focus of the check-in conversation should be about the two of you and your relationship, not the kids, the schedule of events for the week, or other topics.

Check-ins should be done six out of seven days. We recommend that couples have a date on the 7th day. A date is a 3-4 hour period of time to have fun together and hopefully to be "skin-to-skin." It is not designed for serious conversations. After all, "on the 7th day we rest," and serious conversations usually do not make for good foreplay.

What Should We Talk About?

The focus of your check-ins should cover topics related to all three members of the YUMMY relationship. The speaker should address:

- **ME:** How am I doing, as a spouse in our relationship or on my personal goals?
- **YOU:** How do I think you are doing on your goals? It is very important to be positive here.
- **US:** How do I think our relationship is doing? How am I feeling about our marriage?

Realistically you cannot both cover all three topic areas in 5-20 minutes. So, pick and choose what is most important. Remember that you can talk about good things, not just issues and problems. Catch your spouse being good, doing well, and succeeding. Praise is usually appreciated.

Conversation Prompts

Some couples wonder what to do if they really cannot think of any issues or compliments. We suggest that they grab a self-help book and read something from it. Even "point, read, and discuss" can be a good start for a quick yet meaningful discussion. Some couples use books of questions or cards like the Ungame Cards. Some use books on sexuality and sexual exploration. We've also compiled a list of YUMMY conversation starters, which you can find in our Appendix.

Weekly Check-ins

Daily check-ins are best when you are in a crisis or recovering from a challenging situation in your relationship. However, some couples choose to modify that plan.

When our children were young and we were feeling distant from each other in our busy lives, we did a weekly check-in. It was a quiet time to talk about whatever was important or bothering either of us. As a shy and passive person at times, I tended to avoid conflictual subjects. This allowed me a time every week to clear the slate.

Whether you're doing daily or weekly check-ins, the check-in process helps you be better able to deal with issues as they arise, before they become problematic situations. This is the tool that has saved thousands of our couples, including our own marriage.

Obviously, couples can have important conversations at any time, but planning for this activity can be a way to structure for success. It can increase your level of comfort and connection, allowing for more harmony and peace together!

Chapter 7

Sex and Sexploration

WHEN YOU THINK about what makes for a great marriage, sex might not be on the top your list. Sure, great sex is nice, but is it critical?

Yes, it is. In fact, Israel and I believe that sexual satisfaction is one of the greatest predictors of a long-term YUMMY marriage. Because of that, we take time during every retreat to focus on a couple's sex life. We urge you to do the same.

Couples need time to be emotionally intimate as well as physically and sexually intimate. No matter what. Even if she is pregnant or nursing; even if he is traveling; even if they are 80 years old. Being sexually active does not necessarily mean having intercourse. It can mean connecting in another intimate way: holding hands, kissing, fondling, a blow job or hand job, or even cuddling.

YUMMY couples want the vibrancy all of the 3 L's. They want to feel loved, liked, and lusted in their marriage. They want comfort, respect, and fun, as well as the excitement and attraction of being "in love." Therefore, they usually want to have more great sex (or perhaps, "good enough" sex) in addition to having a loving and trusting relationship. Couples of all ages can enjoy their physical connection together. Even elderly couples can enjoy a "bare, naked snuggle" time together.

Sexual Problems

Sexual problems can destroy even a good marriage over time. A low-sex, problemed sex, or sexless marriage usually points to other problems as well. It is not just about the sex. On the other hand, good sex in a healthy relationship leads to greater happiness and is one of the best affair prevention tools.

Human sexuality is an extremely complex subject and is, for many couples, a very tender and sensitive topic. It is private and personal. Sadly, most therapists rarely inquire about a couple's sex life or know what to do to help couples improve or resolve sexual concerns. Many therapists avoid the subject completely because of their inexperience with the subject or their personal discomfort.

In our practice, Israel and I are very comfortable dealing with the subject. We've found it is essential to explore the topic of sex and sexuality. It is important that couples find common ground and that they heal from past sexual wounds. Guided discussions help to create healthy and mature connections in a couple's current sexual relationship together and to heal wounds from this relationship and from past relationships. Many couples have different levels of libido and interest in sexual experiences. We help them to bridge their gaps.

So, let's talk about sex!

It Takes Two to Tango

Most people know that emotional intimacy can lead to sexual intimacy. It is also true that sexual intimacy can contribute to emotional intimacy and to an emotional connection. Think about "pillow talk," that emotionally close time after sex of snuggling and talking. It helps build the bond of love for many couples.

However, men and women often bring their own distinct social conditioning and hang-ups into the bedroom. Understanding these can help you understand the sexual component of your relationship, as well as lead to interesting conversations and plans for a better future.

Men and Sex

Men are socially conditioned to be more selfish and out of touch with their vulnerable feelings. The macho stereotype talks about how big boys don't cry—they are encouraged to have poor impulse control and to need immediate gratification.

For many men, sex is how they feel loved and how they feel alive. It is a vital sign and can be a physical urge or need. Therefore, if they are not sexual with their wife, they will probably find that opportunity with another woman. Perhaps they will turn to pornography as a way to avoid seeing a prostitute or having a full-blown sexual affair. Either way, their needs will likely be met elsewhere or they may sublimate to other activities like becoming a workaholic or exercise addict.

Surprisingly, men are often more sensitive to feelings of rejection, inadequacy, and shame than women. If they are feeling unwanted or undesirable, or are having sexual functioning challenges, they will consciously or unconsciously stop initiating any sexual activity. When a couple is not having much sex or is completely sexless it is almost always the man's decision or behavior, not the woman's.

It makes sense if you think about it closely. Men's genitalia is "out there for the world to see." They cannot fake an erection. They cannot fake an orgasm. Women can, and sometimes do.

Women and Sex

Women are socialized to be the caretakers in a relationship, to control their needs, delay their gratification, and avoid asking for what they might want sexually and in other relationship situations. Popular culture would have you believe that women are not interested in sex and often will fake a headache or other ailment to avoid having sex. This is not usually the case.

Another misconception about women is that they can have an orgasm through intercourse alone. The reality is that most women need some kind of clitoral stimulation in order to achieve an orgasm. Usually a vibrator or fingers are needed to get the job done. Oral sex can bring with it another layer of issues both good and challenging. Remember, attraction is often associated with taste and smell.

Mystery and Excitement: Critical Ingredients

While emotional connection and closeness is essential in a committed relationship, too much closeness (and too little mystery) can sabotage the achievement of a juicy love life. Love and lust are strange bedfellows, and being too familiar with your partner can squash your sexual attraction and desire. This is one of the great challenges of a long-term, YUMMY relationship.

Dealing with the everyday life of diapers, bills, or dishes can be a mood crusher and interfere with lusty attraction for both partners. Couples need some distance—some unknown and hidden aspects to their life—in order to kindle sensual or lustful sparks.

Psychotherapist and author Esther Perel talks about the need for exciting and playful struggles in order to keep a marital sex life alive and vital. Common beliefs about the need for equality, togetherness, and total honesty can damage a healthy sexual and erotic attraction. They actually can kill a sexy mood. Couples need some mystery, excitement, and fun to tap into their erotic connection.

It can be a challenge to feel close, safe, and loved while also being excited for each other. Sex in a committed relationship needs to have just the right balance of: security, trust, and safety, as well as curiosity, excitement, and surprise.

Lust in Long-term Relationships

As your relationship progresses, newness and excitement will ideally transition into comfort and commitment. Now, with established trust and confidence in the relationship, limitless and unbounded exploration and experimentation are possible. This can be the doorway to a new deeper level of excitement and *sexploration*.

Take a moment to remember:

- The thrill of your first kiss together with your spouse
- Your first hot love experience together
- Sex in exciting new and different locations

In the early stages of a relationship most couples are excited about their partner, attracted to them, and turned on by the thrill of having a new lover. You do not need any other stimulus. At the same time most people who have vivid sexual fantasies are not comfortable sharing them with new partners for fear that they will be seen as a pervert and their partner will run for the hills.

However, in a long-term committed relationship, partners should be comfortable sharing their fantasy thoughts and what some people call "kinky desires." Just because you have wild thoughts that excite you, does not mean that you want to (or need to) act on them. Just using dirty talk can be enough to bring a spark back into the bedroom.

Sex does not have to be cubby-holed into boring old vanilla or wild-crazy-kinky sex. Utilizing fantasy role-plays, dress up, or light BDSM such as spanking or dirty talk can be a fun alternative. We have coined a term to describe this playful zone between vanilla and kink as "mocha sex."

One of the advantages of years of training in psychodrama training is that Israel and I enjoy trying on different roles. It is fascinating how some behaviors that seem uncomfortable in ordinary reality can be fun and exciting when you are playing a role of someone else or a character. We call this "role expansion." It is a way of getting out of your comfort zone and being playful.

Fantasy

Monogamy can be boring. One of the ways of dealing with the desire for having new and exciting sex partners is the use of fantasy within the marriage. The idea is to build anticipation, much like you had in the early days of your relationship, as well as having some fun and excitement during sex.

Fantasy is one of the techniques used by long-term married couples to keep things alive and fun, and for older couples to keep "things" up. It is a way to spice up a marriage without the risks of blowing up and destroying the marriage. Fantasy lets each person explore his or her own personal goals and sexual boundaries within the limits of a commited and monogamous marriage.

It is also a way to bridge the gap between what one person wants sexually and what their spouse wants. If the husband is interested in anal sex and his wife is not interested, she can say "shove it in my ass." He can imagine it happening without it happening in reality. His body and mind can be turned on by the thought or image of this desired sex act, while respecting her boundaries. Of course, couples need to strike this agreement and be clear about personal boundaries before having sex.

Fantasy Versus Reality

While fantasy is fun, it's important to remember that there is a difference between fantasy and reality. Couples in their 20s and 30s often have difficulty keeping fantasy firmly in the make-believe world. When a guy says that his biggest fantasy is to have two women in bed, his wife may take him literally and feel pressured to provide her husband with his dream scenario.

While it may be something that turns him on in his fantasy world, he may not actually want or need for it to happen in reality. For many women it can be a very painful lesson to learn later that she did not have to follow through in reality. The fantasy itself would have been good enough. Some sexual adventures in reality can have damaging consequences to the relationship and should be considered with caution.

> **YUMMY Food for Thought:**
>
> Have you ever used a role-play to enhance your sex life with your partner, such as: doctor/nurse, professor/student, babysitter/parent? Did any go really well? Did any flop? What are some fantasy role-plays that you've been wanting to try?

Open Marriage

In 1972 the book *Open Marriage* by Nena and George O'Neill hit the bookshelves hard. The book's primary purpose was encouraging the value of having some space for individual personal growth in a marriage with role flexibility and equality. Most readers, however, focused on the 20 pages that talked about the possibility of sexual exploration with new partners outside of the marriage. While that was not the focus of this book, it did encourage an exploration of forbidden activities at that time. It started a sexual revolution.

During this period Israel and I were both married to other people. Each of us was swept away with the excitement of this open marriage concept. It allows for the opportunity to have the safety and security of marriage with all of the benefits of being single. It was a win-win, or so we both thought.

For many years, I regretted marrying my first husband. He was a great guy, and I loved him dearly. We probably should have lived together without ever marrying, but his Catholic parents did not like that idea.

We ended up living like best friends, and in essence we both kept dating other people. I think that for a young couple, it is a way of making a semi-commitment not a full commitment. It is a way to have some support from a good friend, cheaper rent, and still be able to "sew oats" or check out some prospects for a future relationship.

Swinging, Swapping, and Polyamory

Some couples enjoy a lifestyle of swinging or swapping partners. They see this as fun and exciting. It can be valuable if you want to explore sex with new partners, new positions, new tastes and smells, or even being with more than one partner at a time. Other couples chose to live in a committed relationship with more than the traditional single partner. Polyamory, which is becoming more common in popular culture, is having many lovers part time or full time.

For some couples these alternative lifestyles work well. But for most people, it is too stressful and cumbersome. We've found that most people feel threatened and are too jealous. A communal lifestyle can challenge people's communication skills and self-awareness. As we say, "You need a black belt in communication to be polyamorous."

Having sex outside the relationship opens up a world of unforeseen trouble. Just like affairs are often painful for the non-participating person, open sexual relations usually create tension for the married couple. Sleeping with other people often has unintended consequences that can blow up the marriage.

Arousal: Getting in the Mood for "Love"

For some couples who feel that they've lost the spark, just the idea of getting aroused and desiring sex with their partner can be overwhelming. Many people find that the best way to feel aroused is to JUST get started. Once they start fooling around they begin to feel some emotional desire and some physical arousal.

Good sex starts with feeling good about yourself. Knowing what you want and need inside and outside of the bedroom is essential. Confidence and self-assuredness, as well as being well rested and nourished, go a long way in feeling attractive.

Ask yourself if you have adequate:

- Sleep. Sleep is underrated!
- Quality time alone to read, walk, do yoga, or have other solo activities
- Time to be silly and playful—both alone, with your spouse, or your friends

All of these will help you to feel peaceful and to spark your desire. Similarly, it's important that your relationship be in a healthy place. While make-up sex has a good reputation, the best sex happens between well connected partners. Ask yourself:

- Are you both feeling good about your relationship?
- Do you need to "clear the air" before you can relax and open up?
- Do the two of you "have a life" together as a couple, separate from kids and friends?
- How YUMMY is your marriage? What do you need to make it better?

Teach Each Other Your Sexual Desires

Most couples need to explore and talk about how they get turned on. It can be a challenging conversation if you are sensitive and feel rejected easily, yet it is a very important one so that you avoid any assumptions. Our society shies away from talking about sex, assuming that couples can just figure it out between the sheets.

Talking about your desires and turn-ons is critical to having a satisfying sex life. To talk about this, you need to know what *you* like. Some people learn about their sexual arousal, desires, and ways to orgasm by masturbating. Others learn when they explore with their sexual partner.

Sexologist and educator Jaiya Ma has some good information on different "Erotic Blueprints." She says that people tend to be: sensual, energetic, sexual, kinky, or shapeshifters (a combination). It can be fun to explore your preferred sexual language and turn-ons. What you like sexually may change over your lifetime, so be open to your changing desires.

It is good to talk about wants and desires when you both have some time and space from ordinary life. It usually is best if you are both out of your bed. Most people do not want a lot of direction while they are in the heat of passion.

Talking about sex is an opportunity to use some of the good communication skills described in Chapter 5. Remember, men can be extra sensitive when it comes to sexual performance. Society says that they are supposed to know everything about sex and be great lovers without any specific training. Be positive and gentle with each other. Talk about what you want and like. Avoid talking about what you don't like and don't want. It makes a difference.

Good sex can be seen as the result of a team building process. Talk about it beforehand (out of bed). "Sexplore" together in bed, or in some other fun place. Then, discuss what worked and what did not work later on. Learn and grow together. It may be very uncomfortable at first, but it will pay off in the long run for both of you.

> **YUMMY Food for Thought:**
>
> What was a great sexual experience with your partner? What made it so great? What is something sexual that you would like to do, but haven't yet tried? Talk about that together.

Healthy Sex, Great Sex

Sex is natural, and sex is fun. It is good for each person's health and well-being. It increases the bonding and connection needed for most married (and non-married, but intimate) couples. It can add years to your life in addition to providing some peace of mind. Sex can be a great form of exercise, as well as a spiritual experience. It lessens depression and anxiety and can put a skip in your step.

Sexual activity can be seen on a continuum: from making love and romantic sex, to recreational fun sex, to lustful animal sex. Many couples get stuck in one style of sexual relations. We often recommend exploring other types of sexual activity to deepen the relationship or add more fun and excitement.

Orgasms

Orgasming is one of the ways that a person can release tension and destress. It's great for falling asleep. I call it the "magic sleeping pill." Laughing and crying are good stress relievers, as are screaming, or extreme exercising. But orgasms just might be the most fun. Many couples see orgasms as "the point" of sex, but there's a lot of fun to be had in the journey towards the orgasm.

Lots of jokes have been made about the difference between men and women when it comes to sex. Some say that getting a woman turned on is like cracking a safe. Three turns to the right, two turns to the left, up, down, softer, harder, etc. And then next week the entire sequence may change again. Yes, women can be more complicated than men. On the other hand, men are so simple and easy, "Touch 'it' ANYWHERE and things will get going!"

Getting to an orgasm can be challenging for many people—male and female—because they need to quiet their brain and focus. Some techniques such as meditation, yoga, or Neurofeedback training can help with quieting the mind. While it can be frustrating to lose an erection during sex, it can actually build up the energy for a better orgasm. Many tantric techniques incorporate a start-stop process to build the energy for a bigger and better orgasm later on.

Be patient. Israel says that getting to an orgasm is like doing Sudoku: it takes concentration for most people. He says that focusing needed for an orgasm is good for exercising the brain. Who knows? It may even prevent Dementia or Alzheimer's!

So, How Do You Get There?

We like to use a scale of 0-10 to show the process to get from start to finish: from no interest in sex, to orgasm.

- Stage 0-3: Flirting and foreplay
- Stage 4-7: Feeling aroused and turned on
- Stage 7-10: "I'm CLOSE" and achieving the Big O

It's important to know what stage you're at, since some words and actions that are a turn-off early in the process can become majorly erotic once you're hot and heavy. Consider the F-bomb. Many people are uncomfortable with that word and would cringe if their partner said the word "fuck" over a fancy dinner. Those same people might get turned on if their partner says "fuck me harder" when they're just about to come.

Knowing where your partner is on the spectrum can help you to build and maintain their arousal. As sex therapists we want to know where the challenges lie so we can explore useful techniques to help out. It is useful to know which words and behaviors turn you, and your partner, on and which ones turn you off—and when.

> **YUMMY Food for Thought:**
>
> What words are a turn-on when you are getting warmed up? What behaviors are a turn-on then? What words are useful when you are about to come? What behaviors are useful then?

Foreplay

Foreplay begins the moment that your last sex session ended. In other words, everyday life should be foreplay. The attraction dance is important every moment of the day, not just 30 minutes before you hope to get lucky. Sorry guys!

Kind words and loving acts can qualify as foreplay for many people. Foreplay doesn't have to be an elaborate production of rose petals and champagne. For many people a sweet look, a warm smile, a loving touch, a hug, a compliment, or a goodbye kiss before work can set the stage.

It could be picking up after yourself, helping around the house, a cup of coffee in the morning, saying please and thank you, leaving a note on your spouse's car, or sending a sweet or sexy text. All of these things are likely to make your spouse feel loved and therefore more open to having sex with you.

Many couples skimp on foreplay to get to the main act: penetrative sex. Remember that foreplay can be critical to great sex for some people. For others foreplay is not needed at all. Good foreplay communicates interest, desire, and attraction, not just via words but by behaviors too. It also prepares the body for what is to come. Often, just feeling loved and appreciated by your partner can be an aphrodisiac even if it occurs hours before the sexual activity.

Kissing

Deep attraction usually begins with looking at each other's face, specifically the eyes and lips. For many people, kissing is more intimate and vulnerable than intercourse. Many people remember the famous scene in "Pretty Woman" where Julia Roberts' character says she doesn't kiss. Prostitutes and escorts that we have helped in therapy sessions say that they never kiss their "date" because they may become emotionally attached and their goal is to keep it as "just work."

Some couples have stopped kissing for various reasons. Maybe he chews tobacco, she smokes cigarettes, or someone does not brush their teeth often enough. A person's breath usually gets staler as they get older. Many couples do not talk about this for fear of rejection.

If "being desired and wanted" is one of the ways that you feel loved and turned on, then kissing is very important to include in your foreplay activities. Kissing can be extremely sexy. It can even be seen as a form of fantasy, like the excitement in a juicy romance novel. If kissing is that powerful, all YUMMY couples should be doing more of it.

Sex in The Real World

It would be great if we were able to connect erotically with our partners all the time. However, the erotic, sexual space gets infringed upon by the obligations of everyday life: bills to pay, deadlines to meet, laundry to do, and kids to raise. Keeping your sex life YUMMY amid all these challenges takes some skill and technique.

Some of the sexiest people are not gorgeous or perfect. They just act confident. Your spouse knows about your extra 10-20 pounds of fat. He or she knows about that mole on your back. Sometimes you just need to fake it until perhaps you actually believe that you are beautiful and sexy.

Scheduled Sex

Almost everyone baulks at the idea of scheduling sex. After all, a schedule is the opposite of spontaneity and fun. Yet, scheduling time for sex increases the odds that it will happen. Many people are so busy with their daily lives that they don't prioritize time to be intimate with their partners.

While spontaneous sex is usually the hottest sex, scheduling time for sex is valuable. Obviously, some "dates" will get cancelled because of life getting in the way, but many more will happen—and that is useful. You plan your dinners and schedule self-care activities, so why not put sex on the calendar as well?

Survival Sex: The Quickie

In most relationships, sex is not *always* mind-blowing and ecstatic. Sometimes, you need to have a quickie, or what Psychologist Barry McCarthy describes as having "good enough" sex. Although quickies might not be as satisfying as long, drawn out sessions, they can help you stay connected with your partner.

Quickies can also be pragmatic. They can help bridge differences in sexual appetites. They can help couples with young children keep a physical connection. For elderly couples and couples dealing physical disabilities, "good enough" sex can tap into the healing power of touch.

Getting Guidance

Some couples need a bit of help getting in the mood. Today, there are many wonderful guidebooks on sexual techniques to choose from. You can start with basic concepts that use slow and gentle touch, and move toward touch that is firmer or harder and faster. Tantric techniques give a distinct experience, while vibrators and sex toys can bring new life into the bedroom. Some couples like to watch porn together—some don't.

Talk with your partner and sexperiment. Some techniques and toys will turn you both on. Some ideas will be great, and others will not stay on the preferred list. What do you have to lose?

Sex is natural, but developing a healthy sex life doesn't always come easily. It is important that couples structure for success in their sex life by planning a weekly date night, exploring their desires, and perhaps by including "quickies" into their sexual menu.

Blowjobs Could Save the World!

I have often said that blowjobs could very well save the world. If more men got a blowjob every few days the world might be a little bit calmer and peace might prevail. Of course, remember that some women may appreciate a sexual servicing too.

Sex and Religion

Many people find that their religious beliefs, or their former religious beliefs, have a negative influence on their sex life. They feel guilt and shame about their sexual thoughts and desires, even if it is only in the privacy of their own mind.

Many people who were raised religiously struggle with feeling some shame connected with their sexuality. Some feel uncomfortable with masturbation; others feel shame about wanting oral sex or anal sex. And other people may feel shame about being attracted to someone of the same gender.

Part of our work with couples often touches on their wounds from childhood related to sexual taboos. We often need to give them permission to explore things that turn them on in healthy and safe ways even if it challenges their religious beliefs and values.

Remember, not all religious teachings frown on sex. Jewish married couples are supposed to make love together on the Sabbath night (Friday) after a well-prepared meal, some wine, and some family fun. Similarly, The Song of Songs is an entire poetry book in the Old Testament that talks graphically about sexual and erotic love.

Safe Sex

Within a committed relationship, sex can be risky physically and emotionally. Outside of a committed relationship, the risks increase even more. Sexually transmitted diseases, urinary or bladder infections, unplanned pregnancies, and other sexual oops can happen to anyone. Believe me, I speak from experience!

STIs and Unwanted Pregnancy

Many years ago, I dated a professor who was a bit wild and crazy. We had a lot of fun together and had some fairly risqué experiences. Unfortunately, one of those "fun" nights led to me contracting *herpes*. Yes, I got a good ol' STI.

I share this as a warning to anyone who thinks that they will not get an STI or get pregnant from a casual sex experience. You can, and you might. Even if you're a clever soon-to-be sex therapist.

It upsets me when I hear stories from our clients about how they contracted syphilis, gonorrhea, Chlamydia, or HPV during an affair and then "shared it" with their spouse. Even worse, perhaps, is when an affair has led to HIV, AIDS, or the surprise "gift" of an unexpected child.

Remember that a simple fun experience can become a profound life-changing event. Be mindful and be smart. As Israel says, "Use two forms of birth control. It could save a lot of heartache and more! And remember to use water-based lubes if you use condoms."

Shaving, Waxing, and Laser Treatments

Hair removal on the vulva has become popular among many women. While it is not of interest to all women, many men find it exciting and fun. However, it can be problematic.

If you decide to shave, wax, or do laser work consult with the person treating you and confirm that it is useful to keep some of the hair "down there." I am not a medical doctor, but I believe that pubic hair can help prevent vaginal and urinary infections, so keep a "racing stripe."

While writing about sexuality for this book, I tried all kinds of hair removal. Unfortunately, I learned about the need for hair, once again, the hard way. If you have ever had herpes (even if you have been incident free for a long time) some professionals recommend that you take a dose of preventative meds so that you do not have a new outbreak from the lack of hair.

Anal Sex

Anal sex is a top fantasy for men, next to a threesome (ménage a trois). To keep anal sex fun and safe, it's good to prepare ahead of time. While the vagina usually offers some natural lubrication, the anal cavity does not. That means you should have tons of lube on hand—more than you think you'll need!

In addition, the anus harbors bacteria. Because of that, it's not recommended to put toys or body parts that have been in the anus into the vagina, since this can increase the risk for an infection. Some people like to do an enema to be extra clean, especially if there is any desire to go ass to mouth or ass to vagina.

This might seem off-putting to some people, but many people find it exciting to get all cleaned up before sex. In addition, the anal area has a lot of nerve endings, so stimulating the area with fingers, safe probes, or a penis can be a positive sensation. Some women and men can have an orgasm through anal play and some women even claim that it is easier to achieve an anal orgasm than a vaginal orgasm. If you're both on board, why not give it a try.

> **YUMMY Food for Thought:**
>
> Are there sexual things you'd like to try but have been afraid to ask for? New "toys"? New words? New behaviors or actions (sexperiments)? New locations or time of day? A role-play? Talk with your spouse.

Chapter 8

Affairs and Infidelity

CONTRARY TO POPULAR belief, most affairs do not begin with lustful attraction for someone outside of the marriage. Affairs are the result of loneliness, a search for meaning in life, a struggle with one's mortality, or the need for more fun and excitement. Typically, there is an internal struggle going on and then an opportunity presents itself.

What typically happens is that someone outside of your marriage listens to you. They see you on a deeper level. They make you feel good about yourself. The attraction builds. The relationship continues as an overclose friendship. This is called an emotional affair.

This relationship may move to a sexual level as well—and maybe not.

Causes of Affairs

Individuals are more likely to look elsewhere for validation when their marriage is under stress and in trouble. If your relationship is too serious, tense, or even boring, you—or perhaps your spouse—might be tempted by the attention and attraction from someone else.

When a couple does not spend enough quality time together their connection and bond are at risk of being broken. This is very common: each spouse becomes busy in his or her own life and they lose that essential focus on their identity as a couple. Traditionally, men become busy with work and projects while women become busy with the children. They both cease to prioritize enjoying quality time together as a couple. You may recall that it even happened to Israel and me many years ago.

If you feel more like siblings than spouses or have fallen into repetitive patterns, the intrigue, secrets, or surprises of a new relationship can be exciting and irresistible. Luckily, we all have some power over temptation and infidelity. YUMMY couples can prevent affairs within their marriages by talking with each other before things go off track. Many couples can also overcome an affair if one has occurred. Sometimes an affair is exactly the crisis that turns a mediocre marriage into an exceptional marriage.

In our busy and over-stimulated world, many people today need some kind of excitement to keep them attracted to each other. Affairs are one way for an individual to find that excitement outside of the marriage when their marriage has started to feel boring and stale. By keeping excitement alive in your marriage you can protect yourself against infidelity.

The Excitement and Thrill of an Affair

The appeal of an affair might be based on a sense of danger, excitement, and thrill. Those risky sensations can make you feel fully alive at a time when you feel half dead in your monotonous daily life. Often, the cheater feels they have found someone who listens and understands them on that deeper level. Sneaking around to meet with them is very exciting.

Excitement is not always about sex. More often, it's about the need for some unpredictable and spontaneous adventures. This is one way to feel young again. It's like when you first met your spouse and were curious about everything regarding your new lover.

Surprisingly, some people who have an affair are happily married. We often hear from our clients that they have almost everything with their spouse and "if they got this one thing from someone else, they would be okay."

The spouse is a good travel buddy or good co-parent, but something is missing: they lack one of the three L's. Perhaps it is sexual in nature, but not necessarily. More often it is actually liking your spouse and feeling liked and "seen" deeply by them. People have an existential need to be "known" on a deep level and if it is not found in your marriage it may be found elsewhere.

Emotional Affairs

When you hear the word "affair" you likely think about sex. Of course, some affairs are based solely on sex. However, more often than not, affairs are about intimacy. That's why the term "emotional affair" has entered our vocabulary in recent years.

Affairs are not black and white. Spouses engaged in emotional affairs are reluctant to stop them because they fully believe that "they are just friends" and "nothing is happening." They need to look at the big picture in order to understand the problems with this inappropriate and overly-close relationship. Then, they must make useful changes to adjust the situation.

Signs of Trouble

As we've talked about, couples often "divide and conquer." It is a strategy for managing the many responsibilities in life including work, school, kids, household projects, and chores. Commonly the husband works outside of the home and the wife tends to the children. Sometimes it is the reverse, but the dynamics are the same.

You probably know, intellectually, that your marriage takes time and work. Perhaps you are distracted by "life" and your marriage has slipped in priority. It now is in second place (or worse) on your priority list. Before you know it, years can pass. You begin to grow apart. You can feel estranged from your spouse; you probably feel lonely. You begin to question your compatibility and potential for happiness together. Your relationship is no longer couple-centered.

During the process of growing apart you are vulnerable to an emotional affair. You may be vulnerable to a sexual affair as well. Trouble begins when one or both partners feel a repeated sense of anger and hurt, or experience a sense of constant disconnection and distance. Partners no longer feel as if they are each other's best friend, lover, and confidant.

Then comes the inevitable comparison of your spouse to someone else. That person looks hot and sexy. They are intelligent. They have a good sense of humor. Perhaps they are kind and able to listen patiently. Now, they have your attention. Unfortunately, these comparisons are solely based on an idealized and glamorized version of this new person. This is an unrealistic comparison to the day-to-day reality of your spouse.

When it comes to sexual activities, comparing affair sex to marital sex is unrealistic and dangerous, but also, it's very common. For most people who have cheated, the affair sex is exciting and seems impossible to attain in their primary relationship, the marriage. To try to capture this sexual excitement, we recommend spicing things up in the bedroom with the creativity of role-plays and fantasy talk as described more in our chapter on sex.

Where's the Line?

A sexual affair is easier to define than an emotional affair. And depending on your boundaries as a couple, there may be a few grey areas around what is or is not a physical affair. Common grey areas include: the use or abuse of porn, kissing someone else, lap dances at a club, or seeing a prostitute. Many men will argue that they used porn or had a lap dance in order to avoid a "full blown" affair with a co-worker or friend.

An emotional affair, on the other hand, is a very complicated situation. It can happen gradually and the potential cheater might not even realize what is happening. The line for an emotional affair is harder to define and perceptions usually vary from the person involved in this over-close relationship and the non-involved spouse.

You may be engaged in an emotional affair if you are:

- Keeping secrets from your spouse
- Talking intimately with someone, when you should be doing that with your partner
- Grooming and cleaning yourself prior to seeing this person
- Flirting and laughing more with them than your spouse
- Feeling guilty or resentful
- Dreading going home to your spouse
- Fantasizing about being with this other person sexually
- Thinking "If only I got along with my spouse as well as I do with _____"
- Trying to connect with old lovers or new prospective lovers

Noticing that you are having an emotional affair or an overly close connection with someone is good. This awareness can be a sign that you truly care about your marriage and your spouse. You know things need to change at home and therefore you can work on changing the situation.

Before you do anything that you regret, stop meeting with this person, if possible, and definitely stop having any meetings in private. An emotional affair can become a sexual affair very easily. Take your realization as a sign to work on your marriage and on yourself. Find healthy and fun things to do alone, with your spouse, and with healthy friends. Devote time and attention to strengthen your marriage. Try some of the ideas presented in this book. That's a good place to start.

Remember: when you play with fire, you can get burned!

Affair Prevention: Our Story

Temptations for emotional and sexual affairs are everywhere, but knowing yourself and creating guidelines and a structure for marital success is very useful for avoiding them.

In fact, one of the reasons we live on a farm in Northern Vermont is to be away from all of the temptations that were around us in the past. When Israel taught college, he felt a lot of sexual excitement and tension with the female students. Eventually, he chose to put aside his lifetime dream of being a professor at a college because he felt very tempted to act on his attraction.

Both Israel and I have personally experienced sexually open relationships and recall how excited we felt by the "thrill of the chase." Because of that, we have agreed to be proactive and have protective boundaries in place for our relationship. Therefore, we avoid potential issues by:

- not attending parties without each other
- not going out with single friends of the opposite sex
- mostly maintain friendships with other couples who are in monogamous committed relationships

If we feel excited by an attraction to someone out in the world, we bring that sexual energy home and back into our life together. We are committed to each other, to our marriage, and to being affair-proof.

Affair prevention is a lifestyle. It is not simply a single thing to do. In essence it is everything that we teach our couples about being couple-centered and investing in their marriage. That's important whether you seek to repair a break in your relationship or to strengthen your bond.

Being a YUMMY couple means that you are two whole people who are connected in a healthy manner, working together and yet able to stand on your own two feet as well.

Affair Prevention & Affair-Proof

Everything covered in this book is designed for affair prevention and to make you affair-proof. Couples can prevent an affair by scheduling quality time together. Couples need a variety of activities together: deep and meaningful conversations to clear the air or plan for the future, as well as exciting and playful fun times. So, when your spouse asks you to go for a ride to the store or for a walk in the woods, say "yes" and enjoy your time together. Sometimes a walk around the neighborhood or drive to the store together has more benefit than you might ever think.

Here's how you, too, can be an affair-proof, YUMMY Couple:

- Spend fun time together on a regular basis, including quality time in the bedroom.
- Reinforce the things that you like about each other (compliment and encourage them).
- Show appreciation.
- Schedule regular times to have proactive conversations about things that you want changed and improved.
- Do not bellyache to friends, family, or co-workers about your spouse's shortcomings.
- Do not confide in someone who could be a potential lover or partner. Affairs usually start as supportive friendships but then move into being a playful relationship with teasing and flirting.
- Do not go out for a drink with a co-worker of the opposite sex if you feel attracted to them.
- Do not get a ride home from the bar with someone that you are attracted to.

Surviving Infidelity

At least half of the couples we work with at Marriage Quest are dealing with the aftermath of an affair. Helping couples survive infidelity and prevent more affairs comprises a good deal of our retreat work.

After an affair, you have an opportunity to address the bigger picture of your relationship and to strengthen yourself and your marital bond. Learning to be a healthy marital team again can be indescribably fulfilling. However, it is hard work. It requires putting your marriage first, sometimes even before your job and your kids.

Couple-centered marriages are not threatened by other friendships, since they can rely on the power of "The 3 L's": love, lust, and like. Couples who have "The 3 Ls" can have fun and enjoy being together; they feel desired and desirable. In these kinds of relationships there is no room for an emotional or sexual affair.

YUMMY couples can feel turned on and excited with people they meet out in the world, or actors and sports figures seen on TV. They feel the attraction and bring that energy back home to the privacy of their own bedroom. Many couples use the thrill in the world to spice up their sex life by using fantasy talk and various role-plays.

You, too, can learn to bring the excitement and sexy energy home and spice up your sex life while increasing your marital commitment and bond. If you are going to be in a committed relationship for many years it needs support and work. At least some of the work can be fun too. This is what we call "affair prevention," and it works!

Chapter 9

Divorce

I WAS JUST 19 when I married my best friend. We were indeed great friends, and we took good care of each other for many years. Unfortunately, he was far more of a friend to me than a lover. For several years we wondered how to move forward in a better direction. We contemplated divorce many times.

When we finally made the big decision after ten years of marriage we celebrated together with dinner and champagne. We celebrated the changes in our commitment to each other, and the love that we felt sure would continue even though we were about to file for a divorce. At the end of the day, we were both happier, and it was the right decision.

While the decision to divorce was a relief, I still remember how painful it was to be "sitting on the fence" for years, trying to decide which choice was the best choice for each of us and for our relationship. In that position, you weigh out the pros and cons. You try even harder to save the marriage. Eventually, you may decide to let go and move on.

DIVORCE

Israel and I have worked with thousands of couples in the darkest days of their lives, grappling with this delicate situation, seeking a glimmer of hope. They come to us for professional support as they work on their decision to stay in the marriage or to get a divorce. Often, they come to us as a last-ditch effort, their "Hail Mary."

As always, relationships and marriages are complicated. What works for one couple may not work for another. Yet, we've seen that many couples who come to us share a common belief: They think that they are not compatible, when in reality they just never learned how to talk to each other, to listen with a compassionate ear, and to negotiate their differing opinions. These are skills that most people can learn, but have never been taught. With the tools we've covered so far in this book, you can come back from the brink of divorce to have a happy, YUMMY marriage.

On the Edge of Divorce

Many of the couples we work with are on the edge of separating and divorcing; some have even filed divorce papers already. And yet, they pause their divorce process, trying one last thing before dissolving their marriage. Often, when a person looks at the reality of a separation or divorce, they realize that divorce is not what they really want after all.

Sometimes, they've moved in that direction because it seemed like their only available solution. They might not realize they have other options, like reinventing and reinvigorating their marriage, and don't have the tools to do it.

In working together with us, undisturbed by the daily details of life, couples come to realize their crisis is not a sign that their marriage is dead. They learn that they lacked good communication and relationship skills. And that their anger and frustration resulted from hypersensitivity, unfinished business, and wounds from childhood. These realizations open up a pathway forward in the marriage.

Once a couple is able to gain insight into what was causing the marital problems, they can add new relationship skills to turn things around. As a result, they leave us with a more positive and hopeful direction, knowing that they will be better able to cope with each other and their life when inevitable stressors arise.

The Decision to Divorce

One of the big questions we ask someone who thinks they want a divorce is, "How would you feel if your partner was happily in love with someone else? Jealous or relieved?"

If they know they would feel relieved, it is probably time to let go and move on. If they would be jealous, they still have some desire to be with their spouse, and it is worth working on the marriage. Sometimes, the answer isn't clear cut, but the question is always worth exploring.

I asked myself this question when our children were pre-adolescent and Israel was annoyingly grouchy. I knew I would be very jealous of another woman in his life, so my decision was to work harder on our relationship and not seek a divorce.

Separation as a Starting Point

Some couples decide to separate as a way to explore their divorce decision. It is a way to try the option of a life apart without a commitment to divorcing.

Separation usually, but not always, leads to a divorce. However, some couples who live apart for a period of time are able to flip things around and get back on a good path. Usually it is because they get some quality therapy and they have a clear agreement. A good Separation Agreement lays the groundwork for the rules of this period of time. It increases the odds that this time will be beneficial and possibly lead to a new beginning.

Regrets About Divorce

Professor William Doherty, an expert on divorce, claims that about 40% of divorcees eventually have regrets about getting divorced. Many divorced people experience a moral sorrow about not having kept their commitment in the face of personal unhappiness. Other people regret that they did not try harder to save their marriage because they really do love and miss their ex-spouse.

The person requesting the divorce usually feels relieved at first and then, about three years later, has regrets. Unfortunately, the spouse who was dumped has usually moved onto a new life by then. Knowing that divorce regret is common, it's important to consider this decision fully and not make a hasty judgement.

Prior to acting on your decision, get a professional opinion by consulting with a reliable counselor who specializes in marriage and divorce options. This is often called "discernment counseling." In addition, try to choose someone who is also comfortable and experienced discussing sex in regard to your marriage. You might regret a divorce, but it's unlikely you'll regret spending time trying to figure out whether your marriage could be saved, what went wrong, and why.

Divorce: The Logistics

Divorce isn't just an emotional minefield. It's also a logistical nightmare. While mourning the end of your marriage you also have to face dramatic changes including separating your finances and assets, moving, and setting custody arrangements for kids or pets. In addition, there are changes in the dynamics between you and your friends, and you and your spouse's family.

This period will always be stressful, but you can reduce stress by working together harmoniously. Look at the divorce as one last team effort rather than a chance to get even. Feeling sad is better than feeling or acting angry and vindictive.

Conscious Uncoupling and Mediated Divorce

Over the years we have observed that the biggest problem with a divorcing family is the stress between the angry parents and the all-too-common process of a litigated, court based, divorce. This is when two attorneys work hard to get the "best outcome" financially for their client. Chaos and struggles are often the result.

Today, there are ways of divorcing with dignity and compassion. Uncoupling with consciousness and love is good for everyone involved. It is better for the children involved and is a good basis for healthier future relationships with new partners. Divorce should not be a war.

If you've decided to move forward with a divorce, contact your local county courthouse and find a good divorce mediator. A mediator helps both spouses come to an agreement, without the need for attorneys or their legal fees. Israel was a senior divorce mediator for years and saw firsthand how much better the mediation process was for all of the family members involved.

In many states you can file your divorce yourselves without any attorneys at all. This is called "pro se" or self-representation. Many states have booklets explaining this process.

Lengthy divorces benefit the attorneys, but they are not usually good for the couple or for the children caught in the middle of the process. It affects them not just during the divorce process but often in their future intimate relationships as well.

Of course, while Israel and I are experienced therapists in dealing with the decision to divorce and the aftermath of that decision, we are neither attorneys nor divorce law specialists. It is advisable to seek independent legal opinion and make sure you are considering the long-term implications of your settlement.

Children and Divorce

Most parents who are getting divorced worry about how it will affect their children. I'm here to tell you: the children of divorce are not as damaged as most therapists and authors would have you believe. Children are much more resilient and flexible than adults, and much more adaptable than people give them credit for.

Yes, children may hope and dream that Mommy and Daddy will get back together again. However, they are also able to handle the changes well if both parents behave themselves. Children are influenced by your emotional state, so control what you show them. Children tend to mirror their parent's mood and behavior. While it is normal to be sad or angry, sobbing or showing rage in front of your children is not useful.

Remember, children can sense the relationship between their parents. Sometimes a peaceful divorce is a better option than the tension and fighting in an unhappy but intact family. Of course, the best thing you can do for your children is learning the skills that will save your marriage and make it better than ever. Regardless of your marital commitment, work to improve your *relationship* together. After all, you may be parenting together for many years to come.

Get Support for Your Children

Divorce isn't always detrimental to kids, but it's still a good idea to get support for your children during and after the divorce process. Guidance counselors, teachers, and even support groups for the children of divorce can be great resources.

The two most important things you can do for your children during divorce proceedings are: listen to their feelings and needs and be kind and fair to your future ex-spouse. That is beneficial to your children, your ex-spouse, and to you.

We urge parents to remember that whether you are married, separated, or divorced you will always be partners in parenting. Why not make your *relationship* the best that it can be for them?

Putting-down and shaming your ex-spouse to your children is known as Parent Alienation Syndrome. It is not good for anyone. Today there are groups to help any parent who thinks their ex-spouse or ex-spouse's family is keeping them out of their child's life.

Whether you feel like you are being shut out or you think that you might be pushing your ex-spouse away, be aware that there is a tendency after a separation and divorce for some estrangement. Be cautious and remember that a healthy relationship with both parents is the best situation for your children.

Divorce and Pet Owners

Pet owners can be challenged by their new life arrangements after a divorce. Some people are very connected to their pets, especially if they do not have any children. Splitting out two or three cats or dogs can be painful and sad. Be aware of your attachment to your pets and be proactive in asking for what you want. If you cannot agree on the settlement arrangement, it might be useful to get help from a divorce mediator or counselor.

The New Normal

Change is the one constant during divorce. Divorce changes a couple's lifestyle, their roles, their friendship circles, and their financial arrangements. It shifts the meaning of everything in their world.

When couples have tried all they could to save their marriage and "failed," the losses and lifestyle changes they experience can be frightening and overwhelming. However, these changes also allow for some new beginnings. It can be an exciting time in addition to being scary and stressful.

It's important to desensitize to the idea of being divorced, work on personal growth, and prepare for a new role as a single or separated person. Learn creative problem solving regarding the many changes and challenges that will occur after your separation. These changes include: raising the children in two single-parent households, dealing with new financial limitations and possibly losing emotional support and social support from some friends, your former spouse, and their family. There are some great books available for divorce recovery support. One that we recommend is Bruce Fisher's *Rebuilding: When Your Relationship Ends*.

Teamwork During and After Divorce

When a couple agrees to work together to untangle their interconnected life, they offer an invaluable gift to each other. It is often a catalyst for personal growth and life-long learning. This is a sign of love and compassion, a love based in respect and friendship for someone you shared a life with. It should not be misinterpreted as a sign of romance or an attempt to rekindle the relationship. Accept it for what it truly represents. Be honest with yourself and your ex-spouse, be clear, and don't be misleading.

Reflecting on Lessons Learned

The crisis of divorce offers opportunity for personal development and useful growth. Through reflection, you can turn pain into healing and failure into learning. This process of understanding "what happened" allows for each partner to be successful in future relationships.

It takes two people to make a marriage work, and it takes two to help it to fail. I don't say this to blame you but to motivate you to understand what went wrong. Our job is often to level the playing field. What was your part, and what was your spouse's role in the downfall of your marriage?

Contrary to most people's beliefs—or hopes—the divorce rate is higher for second or third marriages. This can be because of the extra challenges of a blended family. It also can be due to the fact that each individual has not learned about good relationship skills and personal self-soothing techniques. They assume that it was "just a bad match."

Learn the skills needed for love and intimacy sooner rather than later. It reduces the chances that bad patterns will be repeated in future relationships.

After your divorce, take time to:

- Learn from this experience. Learn some skills to calm down, relax, rebalance, and find your peace of mind.
- Choose to develop some friendships now, while choosing to postpone other relationships for later.
- Find a new support system separate from your ex-spouse and their family.
- Plan for new roles such as being a healthy single parent, returning to school, or reentering the job market.

On a Hopeful Note:

We have witnessed many couples who worked through their plans to separate or divorce, only to change their minds and decide to work on rekindling their marriage instead. Sometimes, looking at the cold reality of a separation and divorce is the catalyst to flip things around. The open and honest communication that happens when talking about divorce can be exactly what was needed to rekindle and re-invent the stale marriage.

While divorce may seem like the ultimate failure, it is not the end of the world. If it is done with love and compassion ex-spouses can be friends again at some point in the future. It is useful to observe a time of severance between getting separated and the next phase, where there is the ability to be friends again. The relationship between divorced spouses will be a new and different relationship that will evolve over time.

A happy divorce is better than an unhappy and argumentative marriage. Try to improve your relationship and you just might save your marriage in the process. If that's not possible, move forward with a respectful divorce.

Remember, miracles do happen.
We see them all the time.

Chapter 10

Parenthood and Marriage

OBVIOUSLY, SOME COUPLES cannot bear children and others choose to live life without children. Many are work-focused, some have pets as their "children," and many like the freedom of a child free lifestyle. Being married without children is a viable option and one that some couples truly enjoy. Parenthood is a big responsibility and one that should be entered into with consciousness and thought. If you're a child-free couple and intend to remain that way, feel free to skip this chapter.

Most married couples have children together and therefore they experience parenthood together. This stage of marriage can open the relationship up to new challenges and stressors. It is important to invest in yourself and in your marriage during your parenting years in order to stay on track.

The purpose of parenting is to raise children to be valuable members of society and functional adults. Hopefully they can be happy, healthy, warm, compassionate, empathic, and loving human beings able to connect with other people, be productive, and hold down a good job. Ideally, they will make a positive difference in the lives of the people close to them and in the greater world around them.

Your Marriage During Parenthood

In regard to your marriage and your life, parenthood is usually the best of times and the worst of times. It involves the miracle and excitement of the pregnancy and childbirth, balanced with the frustrations and sleepless nights, the joy of seeing your child accomplish goals and dreams, as well as the pain and sadness of watching them fall and hurt themselves or get their hearts broken.

I call parenthood "the 20-year detour" because it impacts the marriage so deeply. Raising children challenges the strength of any marriage. To survive parenthood with your marriage intact, you need to be couple-centered, giving your marriage the attention and nurturing it deserves.

Being child-centered or work-centered can cause extra stress on your marital relationship as well as on your child. It's also poor modeling for your kids. Obviously, children need attention and guidance, but many parents today spend too much time and energy on their offspring and not enough time on each other and themselves.

Marital Problems Affect Kids, Too

Arguing or having a stressful household can have a negative impact on your children, creating anxiety and even contributing to physical ailments like earaches or headaches. Even when parents think that their children are sleeping, sometimes the kids hear everything. While it is good for children to hear peaceful negotiations between parents, mean arguments can create major stress for kids. Next time you're tempted to snap back at your partner, remember that you're affecting your children as well. They are listening to you even when you think they aren't.

If parents argue around their children, then the child's job changes from discovering who they are to saving Mommy and Daddy's marriage. In addition, fighting influences a child's expectation of what relationships should be like. Be a good role model: show your children a kind and loving relationship. Don't be too needy and don't hover too much. Being overly close can be as wounding as being neglectful.

Other Adult Role Models are Important

Positive and loving parents cannot be replaced, but they cannot be the only support for a child. Children need good adult "friends" to help them navigate their life. All children should have additional adults to help out—these can be neighbors, aunts, uncles, grandparents, and friends of their parents. Maybe it really does "take a village to raise a child." This is a win-win. Your children get the benefit of additional positive role models in their lives and you get time to enjoy being couple-centered.

Parenthood Past and Present

When I was growing up on suburban Long Island, kids would walk down the block and gather up some friends to go outside and play a game of stickball or hide and seek. We would spend hours just figuring out the rules to a new game that we were inventing. We were creative and resourceful without any adult assistance. We spent more time outside in nature than most kids today.

Today kids are driven from their soccer game to ballet practice to piano lessons. They participate in structured activities, but have little time for the unstructured play that is so important for a child's healthy development. Many of the skill-building experiences that were part of the past have been lost today.

The job of the parent is to help their child to learn who they are and who they can become, to help them learn the skills of critical thinking and good decision-making. How are kids supposed to learn self-awareness, negotiation, and communication when parents hover over them and make all of the decisions for them?

Hovering over kids can be harmful in the long term, creating anxious adults who are insecure in their decision-making skills. By stepping back, you're allowing your children room to grow and develop. Plus, you're reserving some emotional energy to focus on your marriage and to become more couple-centered. It's another win-win!

Families Today

The fast pace of life today, changing values, technological advances, easy mobility, and increased expectations have added to the creation of confusion and the disintegration of the structure of the family. More than ever, families are uncertain of their ability to care for their members. Many are unaware of the potential rewards that can come from one's family life.

What Has Changed?

Families are more isolated these days from sources of emotional support and practical help. Often, adult children move far from where they grew up. The extended family is less common than in the past. Grandparents, aunts, uncles, and cousins often live far away and are uninvolved.

Today it is common for both parents to work, or for one parent to be away for work regularly, like during military service. Some families have a single parent because one parent is deceased or uninvolved. Many parents are divorced and have children from two or more marriages in one household. Some families are headed by a single parent or by grandparents. These families have extra challenges, but all families are challenged to be strong and to support each other as the family members each grow and change.

Obviously, it is ideal if there are two parents who are physically and emotionally present to help raise the child or children. Being a single parent or acting as one has many challenges. Extended family and a network of friends can help meet some of the childcare needs.

Some Parenting Suggestions

In general, it is good to foster a climate of exploration and safety for children, while creating healthy boundaries that are somewhat flexible. Children need some limits. Limits make us feel safe. While children need limits, they also need the freedom to explore their world and make their own mistakes. If parents micromanage their child, that child will grow up with anxiety and insecurities about what they can and cannot do on their own.

We tell our couples that it is useful to listen and mirror back to a child what they are thinking and feeling, instead of telling them what they should do or how they should feel. These are the same active listening skills we teach our couples.

Old time parents used to say, "You shouldn't feel_____" That just shuts down the child. It is much better to mirror back and encourage them to explore their feelings and decisions by saying something like, "So you feel_____" or, "So you really think you can sleep at your friend's house tonight and do well on tomorrow's exam?"

Being on the Same Page

Being on the same page does not mean that the parents agree on everything or have had a secret meeting to work it all out before presenting a unified front together. It means that Mommy and Daddy are kind and considerate of each other and respectful of their different opinions. They are open to sharing those differences without negative judgments.

It is important to realize that parents do not need to agree with each other, but that they need to be respectful of their differing opinions. In reality, it is actually useful when parents have their own unique values and beliefs and can share those different points of view in a positive way.

Children can better explore who they are if parents are two different people with a range of priorities and perspectives. If both parents are risk takers and "Johnny" is shy and anxious, he may be pushed to do things out of his comfort zone. If "Suzie" loves to climb trees and her parents are low risk takers, this may stifle her creative exploration, and she may be prone to taking risks when Mommy and Daddy are not around. Open conversations and seeking a balance of perspectives is key.

Discipline Versus Punishment

Discipline should not be punitive unless a real danger exists. Once again, good listening is the best approach. Lecturing, threatening, preaching, shaming, blaming, and punishing usually make a child feel angry and in turn become rebellious toward the parent. It can make kids feel worse about themselves and begin a process of disconnecting from any possible positive authority figure.

It is far more useful to foster a climate of two-way discussions, clarification of values, problem solving, critical thinking, and shared decision-making. In the end you may be the person to make the decision, but it is useful to engage your child in the process. Tolerance and acceptance of differing opinions and beliefs are good life skills and improve a child's self-esteem.

From time to time, parents can make mistakes. Therefore, be a good role model and admit when you are wrong or made a mistake. This helps children to feel normal, human, and open to learning from their own mistakes. No one is perfect. When your child does something wrong or makes a mistake, deal with the behavior and event, but don't criticize them as a person. That will help them to learn right from wrong without increasing their shame or diminishing their sense of worth.

Guilt can be useful and healthy. Shame is toxic and damaging. It is far more useful to say things like, "Johnny, I'm really disappointed that you played ball in the house. We've talked about that before because things can get broken," vs. "Johnny, what is the matter with you?"

Parenthood Education

There are many good books available on parenting and parenthood. Some talk about conscious parenting, mindful parenting, or effective parenting. The most important skill that a parent can learn is to be a good listener. Children usually do not need lectures. They need to be truly heard and guided from the place of empathy and understanding.

My favorite book on parenting is called *Parenting: A Skills Training Manual* by Louise Guerney. She is the wife of the man who developed Relationship Enhancement: the communication skill process that we teach to all of our couples. Her techniques are simple and clear. I recommend getting the book from their non-profit organization, The National Institute of Relationship Enhancement.

While good parenting is obviously important, remember that your marriage needs to be nurtured for the best impact on your children. Your love and affection for each other will "trickle down" to your kids and grandkids, making an impact that lasts generations.

Recipes for Family Living

Many years ago, my mother started writing a book called *Recipes for Family Living* as a fundraiser for one of her volunteer projects. I've included some of her ideas on parenting in an Appendix in the back of this book. Some of them are pretty clever!

Chapter 11

Becoming a YUMMY Person

THE NEXT TWO chapters are a blueprint of how you can work toward being a better person and a healthier individual. Try some of the YUMMY "exercises" included.

Strive to be your healthiest and best self. Learn to become a YUMMY person and work towards building a YUMMY marriage for you and for your family.

What is a YUMMY Person?

A YUMMY person:

- Knows who they are
- Has done some personal growth work
- Nurtures self-awareness and self-love
- Knows how to calm themselves down
- Knows what is really important to them
- Has some peace with their past

- Understands their emotional triggers
- Has some distance from their childhood family

Awareness of Your Past

We all have a history, whether we've stopped to consider it or not. On our retreats we talk about "The 90/10 Principle": 90% of your hurt comes from your past, while just 10% comes from your marriage today. If you have insights into your past wounds, you are better able to heal them. You will not blame your spouse for your feelings or act defensive.

This isn't to say that your parents are to blame for everything. Remember that they were likely doing their best, based on what they themselves experienced as children. Still, understanding the influences of your childhood and family-of-origin can help you better understand yourself. Most importantly, know that when you "reparent" yourself and each other, you can heal those childhood wounds, build a stronger marital bond, and improve your self-esteem and your partner's.

Issues of Trust

We all have certain skills to master at different life stages, according to Developmental Psychologist Erik Erickson. If we do not master them when we are young, then we should expect these challenges to reappear over and over again as problems later in life.

The first and most important challenge of human development is to develop trust. This is a foundational task. Feelings of trust (and mistrust) are usually based on early life experiences. This happens in infancy, before a child has language skills. If an infant's needs are met, they will learn to trust the world. They will be better able to bond and attach in future relationships.

Being a preemie, or needing surgery early in life and being separated from Mommy can lead to an unconscious mistrust. Even experiences that happened while you were in utero, like a parent's drug use or conversations around adopting out, can affect the trust or mistrust you have for the world. Any stress you experienced in the womb can set up an unconscious pattern of fear and mistrust that lasts a lifetime.

These feelings will likely rear their ugly head if your partner violates your trust. An affair or even a minor lie can tap into your inherent feelings of mistrust. Current relationship issues may create a sense of abandonment, worry, and danger, which is only magnified by your early childhood experiences. It is a reaction today to triggers from past traumas.

Many people dealing with trust issues in their relationship today do not realize that this was a problem in their early childhood years. They assume that this is the first violation to trust that they have ever dealt with. We often need to explain how trust issues earlier in life probably impacted them, even if they don't remember anything about those early violations of trust.

Once someone realizes that this is true, they can accept that some of their feelings of hurt, anger, rejection, betrayal, and despair were not caused by their partner's deceit, but were triggered and deepened by it. People might also realize they don't have any clear language for their pain since they did not have words for these feelings as a very young child.

Separating from Your Family-of-Origin

Your family-of-origin consists of your parents, siblings, grandparents, aunts, uncles, cousins, other birth relations, even step-siblings, step-parents, half-siblings, or foster siblings and parents. We learn a lot about who we are and what is important to us by understanding more about our childhood family and where they came from, literally and figuratively.

An important developmental step for yourself and your marriage is to distance yourself from your parents and siblings. Family Therapist Murray Bowen describes this independence and separation from family members as "differentiation." It is the ability to be strong in oneself, know what you are thinking and feeling at any moment, be objective about the situation, and be detached from other people's opinions. Differentiation allows you to live your life without your family members influencing all of your decisions.

Our ethnic, religious, and cultural background influences who we are and how we think and feel as well—sometimes more than people realize. Culture and religion often have a big impact on our beliefs, including how we perceive the role of a husband or a wife, the acceptable behaviors for children, family closeness or distance, comfort in risk taking, and norms of sexuality. Examining your family-of-origin can help you understand your perspective on these topics.

> **YUMMY Food for Thought:**
>
> Are their certain roles that are expected of you as a wife or husband related to your cultural or religious background? Are there any that you have rebelled against? Are there set rules from your family-of-origin regarding expectations for closeness and certain family time together, such as holidays, birthdays, vacations, weekends, Sundays, or the Sabbath?

Looking at Your Roots

There is a lot to be learned about ourselves when we study our family roots: the stories of our grandparents and their parents, our family's history, their journey to America or Canada or wherever, the struggles they dealt with here and in the old country, perhaps how some died in tragic situations. Maybe some ancestors were war heroes or famous authors—maybe some were alcoholics or did jail time.

Hearing the stories from long ago can help us to understand some of our own personal struggles as well as our strengths. Understanding the patterns in life that they passed on for generations can help us understand ourselves better, and can help us to feel empowered to make new choices.

Anxiety, depression, and reactions to stress often follow patterns in families. Sometimes wounds of the past seem to live on in current generations. Understanding the family wounds and traumas, as well as their hopes and dreams can bring insight, clarity, and perhaps some relief that you are not the cause of all of your challenges.

It is clear that "hurt people in turn hurt other people." Understanding the drama and trauma experienced by our relatives can help shed light on our own life challenges. Connecting the dots and realizing if there is a family pattern or a "life script" we may be following can be very exciting and transformative. It can allow us the opportunity to make new choices and have a new path.

Many people whose parents came through the Depression Era have a wound around money and food shortage. Some of them became very cautious around food saying things like, "Finish everything on your plate," or "There are people starving around the world." These statements are remnants of past experiences that may seem illogical in today's world.

Family Mishigas and Secrets

All families deal with challenges, stress, conflicts, and a bit of chaos, or what Israel calls "mishigas." Mishigas is a Yiddish word that warmly captures the general craziness in any situation. Israel dealt with a lot of mishigas in his childhood and it impacted how he felt about himself and his childhood.

In an extreme form, a family or community's mishigas causes Adverse Childhood Experiences (ACE). The more negative experiences (ACEs) a child has, the more apt they are to experience addiction and deal with challenges in relationships of all kinds throughout their lifetime.

Situations like this set up a foundation for feelings of shame and low self-worth. Shame is a toxic feeling that says, "I am not lovable or worthy of love." Healing childhood shame is essential to a happy marriage and a happy life.

Shame is closely tied to secrets. Families keep secrets because they are ashamed of something. Confronting family secrets can let you break the cycles of shame. Secrets about adoption and biology, affairs, criminal records, addiction, and mental health are common.

> **YUMMY Food for Thought:**
>
> Reflect on your family. What secrets did your family keep? How have they affected you? What secrets are in your current family? Do they need to be kept as secrets?

Your Lifescript

We do an intake interview with every couple we work with. It is a wonderful experience for most people to tell their life story and family history, and to be witnessed by their spouse and by the two of us. I invite you to do your own intake interview.

> **YUMMY Food for Thought:**
>
> Tell your story. Grab a journal and jot down your answers to the following. Consider sharing them with your spouse or with a good friend. This can be a very powerful exercise.
>
> - Talk about your mother. List three of her positive characteristics or traits and three of her negative characteristics or challenges.
> - Did she work outside of your home? When and what did she do?
> - Talk about your father. List three of his positive characteristics or traits and three of his negative characteristics or challenges.
> - Did he have a job? What did he do? Any periods of unemployment?
> - Talk about your parent's relationship when you were a child and teen. Did they fight? Did they divorce? Did they hug and kiss much? Were they flirtatious or complimentary with each other?
> - Did they give YOU many compliments? Did they hug and kiss you?
> - Did they hit or spank you excessively?
> - Did they try to control your decisions rather than letting you find your own way?

- Did you make any pacts with yourself when you were young about becoming an adult, a parent, or a spouse, such as, "When I grow up I will___ (or I will never___)"
- Describe your brothers and sisters if you have any. Include any that are deceased, including miscarriages or stillbirths. Include step or half siblings if they are significant in your life. Cover details including: their age, marital status, career, children, and where they live. Are you close to any of them today? Are you emotionally cut off from any of them today? Why?
- Did you grow up with any religion? What was its impact on you?
- What is your cultural-ethnic background? Where did your ancestors come from? How many generations back? Do you know any stories about life in the old country? About their transition to their new homeland?

Healing Childhood Wounds

**When marriage is done right
you get to heal your childhood wounds
through the marital relationship.**

We've seen it happen!

To be a psychologically healthy person and be part of a YUMMY marriage, you need to identify and heal your childhood wounds and your early life traumas.

Even in the healthiest of families, a child is wounded. People are not perfect, and parents are people with their own issues and personal challenges. Individuals who thought that their childhood was "wonderful" are often confused later in life when personal or relationship problems arise.

They assume there is something wrong with them when they're having troubles after having a *seemingly* perfect upbringing.

Some social scientists say that the mere cutting of the umbilical cord at birth, the "separation from the mother," is an inevitable psycho-spiritual wound experienced by all human beings. Many religious and spiritual leaders say that our earliest wound is a separation from the creative life force: the divine being, God.

This creates our first existential dilemma: the separation of I and Thou. The desire to reunite and "become one" or "whole" once again is a theme that can be a powerful force throughout a person's life. Marriage mirrors back the paradox of an individual's desire to be one with their spouse, while fighting to be a whole self-sufficient and a distinct individual. Being in the present moment ("in the here and now") in your marriage is a gateway to an existential peace of mind and a greater joy in general.

The Role of Trauma

Many couples we work with struggle with the effects of old traumas. This is typically referred to as Post Traumatic Stress Disorder (PTSD). Even if it is undiagnosed, the effects are real and powerful. Often current traumatic events trigger the unresolved pain of past experiences. This can lead to major challenges and trust issues in the here-and-now. If the reaction to a present-day event seems much bigger than an expected response, it may be because of old unresolved wounds and feelings of shame.

Israel and I help our clients to connect past traumatic events to their current reactions. Often clients experience major relief in knowing that today's events are not as bad as they seem, but are really a triggering of past wounds.

YUMMY Food for Thought:

During the intake process we ask each person about their life traumas. Grab a journal book, and consider what traumas you've gone through. Start with your conception and go up until today, listing "Big T" and "little t" traumas you've endured. These are according to your perception of the event. Sometimes an event that was "no big deal" to one person is huge to another person. Ask yourself:

- Were you wanted as a baby and child?
- Was Mom a smoker or drinker during her pregnancy with you?
- Any accidents or major events during that pregnancy?
- As a kid were you fat, skinny, short, tall, big nose, wear glasses?
- Were you bullied in your childhood? Were you a bully?
- Any childhood sexual abuse, rape, or other sexual violations?
- Did your parents argue a lot or have a bitter, angry divorce?
- Were there any traumatic illnesses or deaths?
- Any major vehicle accidents or scares?
- Miscarriages? Abortions? Difficult pregnancies?
- Bad break-ups? Affairs? Bad divorces?
- Anyone fired or laid-off from a job?
- Any suicides, suicide attempts, significant deaths, or almost-deadly experiences?

Building A Healthy Future

Once you've come to terms with your past, it's time to work towards a healthy future. Take steps forward today for your overall health and wellness. A healthy body helps to contribute to a healthier person and ultimately to becoming a YUMMY couple. It is very useful for you to work on your overall well-being as a couple in addition to making efforts as an individual.

Take A Deep Breath: You can start with the simple, yet profound and essential step: breathing. Learning to breathe deeper and more fully can help with basic wellness by getting oxygen to more cells. Breathing serves as a calming and self-soothing technique. It lowers blood pressure and promotes stress management. So, remember to breathe, slowly and deeply.

Naps and Downtime: Once, I was visiting my cousin, who struggled with addiction and mental health issues. He usually looked exhausted, but this particular day he looked fantastic. I asked him, "What changed?" and he told me he had begun taking a nap, or at least some downtime from the busy-ness of life each day. I was so impressed that a 20-minute break in the afternoon could be so visibly useful. Consider having some shut eye or downtime daily, even if only for 5-20 minutes.

Sleep: Unfortunately, many people today are sleep deprived. This can lead to irritability and relationship problems. Doctors recommend that most adults and college students get eight hours of sleep—children and teens should get even more. That can be challenging to do with all of the daily demands of normal life. However, if you can get more sleep, you can improve your health—and maybe even save your marriage.

Health and Wellness Check-up

In order to consider yourself a whole person, you need to consider your physical health and your overall wellness. Evaluate your strengths and challenges when it comes to your body, mind, and spirit. They all have an impact on your ability to live a YUMMY life.

YUMMY Food for Thought:

During the intake process we ask each person about their health and wellness. Ask yourself the following questions:

- When was your last physical? Do you have any medical concerns or conditions? Are you on any medications? How do they impact your life?
- How do you feel within your body? Do you need to lose or gain a lot of weight? Do you get a good night's rest?
- Do you have any concerns about substance use or abuse for yourself or anyone you love? This can include alcohol, cigarettes, prescription drugs, food, sugar laden or deep-fried foods, or anything else that interferes with your health and wellness.
- How is your mental health? Are you overly anxious? Depressed? Suicidal? Do you worry about the mental health of any of your loved ones?
- How's your libido? When was the last time you masturbated? Had partnered sex? Are you satisfied with your sex life?

Substance Use and Abuse

Everyone has a relationship with mind-altering substances, whether it is alcohol, cigarettes, prescription meds, pot, illegal drugs, heavy foods, or the beloved chocolate bar. Even healthy activities like exercise can become addictive and counter-productive when taken to an extreme.

No matter what your vice of choice is, you should ask yourself whether your relationship with it is healthy or not. Some people can drink moderately while some cannot. Some people can take Valium or pain pills as needed, while others tend to abuse these medications.

Everyone should evaluate for himself or herself if their relationship with each substance is reasonable and useful. Drugs have their purpose, but people sometimes abuse a beneficial substance and find that the substance begins holding power over them. If you question your substance use and wonder if it has become excessive ask a friend for their opinion or consult with a counselor or your doctor.

Evaluate your relationships with different substances by asking yourself:

- Are you using alcohol or drugs to control your physical or emotional pain?
- Are you using a substance to avoid intimacy and closeness?
- Are you using it just to have some fun or excitement?
- Are you using it to feel more alive or to have a deep spiritual experience?

Some people say that any mind-altering substance is a crutch and that people should tough out difficult times without any medications or interventions. I like the analogy of crutches because crutches are commonly used for a period of time when someone has broken their leg and needs some support. They won't use the crutches forever, but they are really useful while the leg is mending.

Some people use alcohol or drugs while dealing with a crisis situation or stressful time. The use of any substance should lessen as the pain of the crisis lessens. We have a motto, "Moderation in all things, including moderation!"

Other Addictions

We often talk about substance abuse, but certain behaviors and activities can also be addicting and can cause deep problems within relationships. Gambling and overspending of money can be devastating to families. Excessive time with technology such as time on Facebook, emailing friends, or playing video type games can feel like a rejection to your partner. Porn can be a challenge for some couples, especially in relationships where one or both partners are opposed to it. Some foods, especially with white flour and white sugar, can be addictive and can be filling an emotional need not being met in your relationship.

These addictions can affect a person's mood, body image, and self-esteem, and thereby impact their intimate relationships. There is a fascinating book called, *Sugar Blues* by William Duffy, that talks about the dangers of sugar and the history and politics of the sugar business.

When dealing with addictive behaviors or substances, it's important to get to the root cause. Why are you using this substance or engaging in a certain behavior? What—if anything—does this say about your level of fulfillment with your life and your relationships?

A YUMMY Challenge:

Try this experiment with addictions. When our kids were young, their elementary school had a "TV turn-off week," during which families turned off the television for one week. It encouraged each family to play games together, go for long walks, check out the local museum, or just talk to each other about their day or about life in general.

Another YUMMY Challenge:

Challenging a habit or routine can force you to try something new, and maybe healthier. Try it sometime: go a week without the TV, without chips or soda, or perhaps without telephones and tablets in your bedroom. You'll notice it isn't easy, but it becomes simpler over time. Reflect on what's challenging and useful during your period of going without.

Mental Health

While all of us face mental health challenges at one point or another, a significant portion of the population lives with lifelong mental illness. People's mental challenges range from mild to severe. Diagnostic evaluations and labels are overused. A diagnosis can be useful for understanding people's behaviors and creating a treatment plan for wellness, but such labels may be limiting and damaging to someone's ability to grow and change.

When one or both spouses has a mental illness, we remind them that the goal of working with us is the same whether they are dealing with any depression, anxiety, borderline personality, bi-polar disorder, or none of the above. The goal is to understand what you are thinking and feeling, and learn how to communicate what you want in a positive and useful manner. These relationship skills are needed by *everyone*, no matter what your gifts or challenges happen to be.

> **YUMMY Food for Thought:**
>
> Grab your journal book and ask yourself these open-ended questions about your health and wellness. See what comes up.
>
> - How are you doing?
> - What are your strengths?
> - What are your weaknesses or challenges?

Defining Yourself: Who are You?

This is an interesting question. Like most people, your first response might be a list of general roles in your life: wife/husband, mother/father, and daughter/son. Then usually it is about your job or hobbies: doctor, lawyer, sales clerk, amazing teacher, yoga nut, or amateur artist.

Too often, we are so caught up in the roles that we haven't taken the time to answer the deeper question of who we are, even to ourselves. If you go deeper, the list becomes more interesting. It may take you to a more existential and spiritual place.

> **YUMMY Food for Thought:**
>
> Try it. Put pen to paper and ask yourself: Who am I, and who do I want to be? Who are you, *really*? An optimist? A pessimist? A risk-taker? Are you this way with money? In relationships? With physical activities? What are your strengths? What are your challenges? Do you like time alone? Do you surround yourself with people? Are you always being busy? Are you judgmental? Are you shy? Are you overly-sensitive? Are you a "Type A" personality? Are you controlled by others' perception of you?

What's the Significance of Your Name?

Although your name was given to you before birth, you have the power and right as an adult to choose a name that has significance to you. Israel chose to return to his Hebrew name, Yisrael, just before turning 40. He experimented with it on a 10-Day retreat. It felt natural and comfortable to him—like a familiar piece of home.

I was Cathleen in my primary grade school classes. Then I was Cathy. I changed the spelling of my name from Cathy to Cathie when I was a young adult. In addition, I often had alternative names for myself as a young child while being creative and playful.

> **YUMMY Food for Thought:**
>
> What's your name? Does it have any great meaning or significance? Do you have a deep connection to it or any feelings about it? In many cultures a person's name carries great importance and history. Does your name tell a story about who you are or who you are meant to be? Were you named after a family member from long ago? Did you change your name or the spelling of your name—when and why? Do you have a spiritual, religious, or secret name? Did you, or do you, want to change your name to something that fits you better? What would that be?

Using Your Voice

Shel Silverstein has a great poem entitled *The Voice*. In it he reminds us that there is a voice inside of all of us. Each of us has a voice inside that talks to us and tries to guide us. Listen carefully. Take notes. Can you hear if there are patterns in your thoughts?

Take charge of your inner dialogue so you are being proactive and not reactive to past messages. Take small steps at a time if necessary. If the messages are old and counterproductive, try to change them. When you learn to take hold of your voice and your life's story, no one can take your power away.

Speaking up for yourself can help you to feel empowered and in control. It is important to learn to use your voice when needed. Stand up for yourself and ask for what you want and for what you need. If the people around you are not listening, try to find a more positive way to share your wants and needs with them. If that does not work, find a good friend or a professional counselor to help you find and strengthen your voice.

While you might not always get to choose what happens to you in your life, you do get to choose the stories you tell yourself about it. You do not need to live by old scripts, stories, or messages from the past. You can "live by choice!" Be the person you want to be. Use your imagination and begin to become your best self. Make an effort to become the YUMMY person that you aspire to be. Be an agent of change for yourself, and turn your marriage around.

> **YUMMY Food for Thought:**
>
> Does your voice sound like anyone else: your parents, your grandparents, your teachers, or your religious leaders? Does it give you good advice, or are you just regurgitating old messages that are no longer useful? Would you speak to a friend the way you speak to yourself?

Support: The Value of Community

In the 1980s, Israel went to a workshop that left an impression on him. Psychologist Joan Borysenko was speaking about the value of having a community of family and friends. She talked about the people in a small rural town in Ohio that had the lowest rate of heart disease in the United States. Amazingly, the people in this community were not on a heart healthy diet or exercise plan. They were beer drinkers, smokers, pie eaters, and many were overweight. The secret to their health was the friendships and the love felt in their community.

Everyone needs to feel loved and supported throughout their life, whether it is from family or close friends. Some people who feel unloved by their family-of-origin decide to have their circle of friends be their family-of-choice. These are the people to turn to when you need a friend. They are your support system or perhaps your play-time buddies.

Some people qualify as your closest friends and you can trust them with anything at all. Other people should be kept at a distance because they have hurt you, or could hurt you in some way. Some friends come into your life for a period of time: perhaps during a crisis moment, while you worked in the same job together, or during a time you lived on the same street together. Other friends are supportive for your entire lifetime.

As you reflect on your community and friendships, ask yourself what you would like from them.

- Who are your closest friends, the ones you trust the most (your inner circle if you made a diagram of concentric circles)?
- Who loves you unconditionally?
- Who would protect you physically?
- Who was there for an important time in your life in the past?
- Who challenges you in good ways?
- Who challenges you in unhealthy and toxic ways?

YUMMY Food for Thought:

Israel went on a vision quest retreat back in the early 90s. One of the preparation questions was, "Who are your people?" We spent several years exploring our answers. I challenge you to consider the same. Who are your people? Who adds positively to your life? Who do you want (or not want) in your community of friends?

Chapter 12

Religion and Spirituality

"DO YOU REALLY believe that God is an old man, with a long white beard, who lives up in the clouds?" Israel asked his Rabbi-Therapist many years ago.

Rabbi Gelberman sat back and smiled thoughtfully while he responded, "That really is *not* a good question. A better question is 'If there is a God, what would he want of me'?"

While many people are focused on the afterlife, what really matters is how our religion and faith affect our life and relationships here on earth, today. If there is a God (or higher power of any kind) how would he or she want you to live your life? What does it mean to you to be a good, kind person? As the Jews say—"to be a mensch."

It seems that most religions teach about kindness, love, respect, and a life of service to others. If you and your spouse come from different religious backgrounds, focus on the common teachings that unite you, rather than the difference in details that can pit you against each other.

Religion can be a place of conflict and struggle when it does not need to be. Wars have been fought for many years because of difference of opinions. Religious debates can be interesting but try to find the common ground with your spouse and family members and don't let your differences pull you apart.

The Purpose of Religion

The purpose of religion is to have guidelines to live by. Many people find comfort in their religious principles, values, rituals, and ceremonies. Other people find rewards in the community support and friendship from a house of worship.

Organized religion may not be right for everyone, especially if it supports beliefs that are in opposition to yours. Many people have rejected their childhood training and religious background. Everyone needs to determine what works for them and realize that their needs may change over their lifetime.

I continue to return to my connection with nature and I strive to be the best person that I can be. Israel and I live in a little piece of heaven where we get to spend hours walking our trails and enjoying our brooks and ponds, while watching the hawks, loons, and herons fly overhead. On occasion we see a bear, deer, or moose passing by. We both find peace and solitude in our connection with nature and all of the beauty that surrounds us.

Spirituality

Spirituality means many things to different people, but most of us have a concept of personal spirituality—some connection to a higher power. Your spiritual and religious backgrounds can inform you on how you approach your family, spouse, and the world.

> **YUMMY Food for Thought:**
>
> Think about how religion and spirituality fit in your world view. What do they mean to you? Is spirituality a missing piece that haunts you, or a place of sanctuary and comfort? Is it a positive connection or a source of disconnect and struggle with your spouse and their family, or with your family-of-origin?

The Power of Nature

Spending time alone in nature, whether it is the northern forests of Vermont or the deserts in California, has always been profound to me. Nature mirrors back life in the moment. It always has answers to my biggest questions.

For a time, Israel and I led backpacking adventures, called "Soul Awakenings" in Vermont, Colorado, and upstate New York. During these retreats, we experienced how nature could help people to:

- Honor the changes in their life—such as after a divorce, a death, entering into a new relationship, or starting a new job
- Heal past childhood wounds
- Clarify their life vision through a mindful exploration of the question of, "What do I want to do next in my life?"
- Make plans for the future and begin a process of transformation

The philosophy of nature-centered activities is that spending time in nature, especially *alone* in nature, can help someone face life's transitions and cycles and enhance relationships with loved ones. It is an opportunity for change and personal growth that relies upon the desire or the need for spiritual attunement and a soulful connection—along with mindfulness and patience.

> **YUMMY Experiment:**
>
> Spend several hours alone outside. You can sit still for a period of time or go for a walk around, sometimes called a Walkabout. Try to clear your mind and just listen. Some say that is what prayer is all about, or perhaps what it is supposed to be about. Just listen. Don't ask or request anything. Just be.

Life's Purpose and Meaning

For some people, life is all about raising wonderful children and grandchildren. For others, it is working in a job to make the world a better place. Hopefully your life has more meaning and purpose than just the everyday to-do list. If not, maybe it is time to ponder life's deeper meaning for you.

Are you more of a "human doing than a human being?" What can you do differently to feel more fulfilled? Often, it's about making your home and work align better with your values and beliefs.

Sense of Place: Where You Live

Sometimes where you live is connected to being the only place you found in your budget. Perhaps it is where there are good schools or is close to someone's job. Ideally, however, you have more of a connection to your home and community than that alone. Where you reside should represent you and your priorities.

Where do you live? In a big city, suburbia, the countryside, near a body of water, with a view of mountains? Each location tells a bit about who you are and what is important to you.

If it does not support your deeper self, consider making some changes. This doesn't mean you have to up and move, though that is sometimes a great idea. Even redecorating some rooms can be the change needed to help you feel "at home" in your place, literally and figuratively as well as practically and spiritually.

Career as a Spiritual Journey

We all need to pay the bills, but ideally your job aligns with your values. Some jobs are stepping stones to future work, and that's okay. If possible, find and take a job that supports *you* and your deeper goals in life. Try to see your career as an extension of your mission in life. If this doesn't ring true, consider making some changes.

Israel and I used to run a program called "Corporate Quest," where we took small groups of employees into the woods to explore their personal and professional goals. Many people, when they reach their 40s or 50s, want more from their job than just a paycheck. They want to feel appreciated and acknowledged for their contribution to the company.

I've had many great jobs over the years, and being a therapist is my life's work. However, one of my favorite jobs ever was being a grocery bagger at the Hanover Food Co-op. It was the least pay I had ever received for a job, but the most rewarding work. I felt like I was blessing people's food and grocery items, not just carefully placing bananas in a brown bag. Sometimes simple tasks are deeper and more spiritual than they seem.

> **YUMMY Food for Thought:**
>
> Does your job fit you? If you could do anything, what would be your dream job? What can you do to get on a path to that job?

Reclaiming the Midlife Crisis

Between the ages of 35 and 50, many people question the meaning of their lives. They have worked hard and acquired or created a family, home, status, and the material possessions that they desired. But then, some doubts arise. People question where they are in their life and where they are going.

Oftentimes, that exploration leads to behavioral changes. Some people become moody or withdrawn. Some turn to alcohol to self-medicate. Others buy crazy things like a bright red convertible. With growing children, hormonal changes, the recognition of one's own mortality, and other factors, this transition can be a dramatic time. This is often when we see a couple for a retreat. One person is expressing dissatisfaction with their marriage and looking for something to change.

This is commonly referred to as the midlife crisis, but we fondly refer to it as a "midlife exploration." By reframing this quest in a positive light, you can use this time to create a life that is more meaningful for you.

A midlife crisis can play havoc with a marriage, plunging a stable family life into chaos and turmoil. A midlife exploration, on the other hand, offers a chance for enrichment and growth. Often it is necessary to dig deeper, to an earlier time in the individual's life, to find significant contributions for their current problems. Finding peace and harmony at this stage of life can allow for a happier transition to one's end of life and eventual death.

Death: The Final Journey

About ten years ago, I received a phone call from the local hospital saying that after reading my mammogram they had some concerns. Israel was out of town visiting our daughter in college. I did not want to burden them, so I was all alone dealing with this sudden and scary news.

After a brief meltdown, I realized that if I had breast cancer and was dying that I would still be doing exactly what I was doing at that moment. I would want to walk the dogs, or go to the pond and watch the ducks paddling around, or sit on a beach chair and read some travel magazines. It was profound to understand that I was actively living my life in a way that felt right to me.

Death is inevitable, and yet many of us are preoccupied with it. We fear, question, and try to control something that is completely uncontrollable. Many people say that the fear of death is actually a fear of having not lived the life that was desired. So, have some fun. Play more. Sing and dance more. Do whatever brings you joy. As one country song goes, "Live like you were dying."

> **YUMMY Food for Thought:**
>
> If you were dying, what would you do differently? What is still on your bucket list of things to do? What do you want the last days and weeks of your life to look like? Is there anyone you need to talk with to clean up some negative past, or to show some unspoken appreciation?

Death and Dying

We all deal with death at some point. Dealing with the death of a loved one can be incredibly painful, but also a chance for growth. Israel and I used to say, "look for the gift in the crisis." Usually it takes a while to understand it all, but if you can find the silver lining, the gift, you can find relief and better embrace the challenges before you.

An expert on the subject, Dr. Elizabeth Kubler Ross, wrote many famous books on death, dying, and the common universal stages of grief. In addition, Dr. Ross also wrote a powerful article called, *Death Does Not Exist*. She talks about her experiences with people who were dying and many of their magical stories. She says that "Nothing in life is a coincidence." Everything happens for a reason. You just need to figure it out, and perhaps look at the situation with a longer lens.

Conversations About Death

Some people fear the dying process more so than death itself. Many people have a fear of death and that process not only because of the fear of the unknown, but because they have not planned for it or talked about it at all.

Talking about death can be difficult, but having a will, a healthcare plan, a financial plan, and clearly-expressed funeral and burial desires helps ease the stress when the inevitable happens. Having clear plans is a gift to the family and friends left behind. Having a meaningful conversation can be very useful and relieving to both husband and wife, as well as adult children. In *The Conversation*, author Dr. Angelo Volandes does a great job of helping people explore and discuss their end-of-life decisions.

> **YUMMY Food for Thought:**
>
> Are your "affairs" in order? Do you have a written plan of what to do if you are sick? If you are unconscious? Your financial plans if you died suddenly? Plans for burial or other final arrangements for your body? Any specific words or readings to be read at your funeral or ceremony of life?

Final Words

I was very lucky to spend quality time with my father before he passed away at the age of 95. Shortly before he died, he recommended the book *Being Mortal* by Atul Gawande. This was the perfect book for me to understand the decision and timing of him going into hospice and the various choices to be made at that time.

I feel so fortunate that I got to spend many years working together with him and Israel developing our Marriage Quest program and on our various websites. I feel particularly blessed that I was able to be with him on the day that he died. He *drifted off* peacefully in his home surrounded by loved ones—just the way he wanted it to be.

Appendix 1

More About Cathie

I WAS BORN Cathleen Barbara Worthing in 1953 in Amityville, New York. Yes, Amityville, the home of the Amityville Horror stories. I never really lived there, only for a couple of days at the hospital.

When I was born, the birth announcement said, "a princess was born". I thought that was a humorous description that all birth announcements had in the 1950s.

Many years later I found out that my ancestors of the 1700s in Hungary-Romania were actually Jewish Kohan (the priestly tribe in Judaism). Well, maybe I really am a princess!!

I grew up on Long Island New York, a Baby Boomer in stereo-typical suburbia—an original Levitt house in the Wantagh section of Levittown. It was a safe and fun place.

I was a cheerleader throughout junior and senior high school. I was in the student organization and President of the Girl's Leader Corp. Like many young gals in the late 60s to early 70s, I went to college to find a husband and to learn about healthy families and more. By January of my freshman year I had a serious boyfriend. We were married a year and a half later.

Today I see myself as a cheerleader for saving marriages and building healthy relationships. I have worked in nursery schools, high schools, and colleges. I worked in corporate Employee Assistance Programs, and as an executive for the Boy Scouts of America. I've worked for three different dating services. I even started one with a good friend of mine, called *To Life!*

Appendix 2

More About Israel

ISRAEL WAS BORN in Bronxville, New York in 1955. His name at birth was Robert Allen Helfand, though his grandparents called him Yisrael. He grew up in Yonkers on the edge of "dah Bronx."

One of his favorite childhood experiences was exploring a nearby park where he dreamed of owning a homestead and raising his own food.

Israel often felt unsafe in school and in his community because of being Jewish. He talks about sneaking out of the schoolyard and running to his Hebrew School classes, hoping to avoid the older Italian boys.

Israel was a "lady's man" though he never really realized it until much later in life. He always had a girlfriend—many of whom were Italian, hence the older Italian boy issues. Israel says that he's always been "lucky in love."

In addition to feeling unsafe around the big brothers of his girlfriends, Israel often felt misunderstood in school because of his learning challenges. To top it off he was a victim of harassment by teachers and administrators because he was Jewish. One of his happiest days was when his father finally acknowledged the persecution and abuse that was going on and stood up to the principal and gym teacher.

Israel is a visionary, a guide, and a teacher. He is a Licensed Marriage and Family Therapist and a Certified Sex Therapist, as well as a Certified Hypnotist. He is well-trained in Psychodramatic techniques. He is intuitive and insightful, willing to take therapeutic risks, and be a pushy pain in the butt at times. In addition to our retreat work, Israel tinkers in construction projects and is a gentleman farmer on our homestead in Cabot, Vermont.

Appendix 3

Conversation Starters

HERE ARE SOME questions and prompts to get the two of you talking. Some are important, fun, or perhaps just interesting. The idea is that there should always be some way to connect with your spouse in conversation. You can also check out some books of questions, Ungame cards, or grab a self-help book off of your bookshelf and read and discuss a paragraph or more.

Pick and choose as desired:

1. Share three things that you are thankful for.
2. What do your friends say about you that you like?
3. What do some friends/family say about you that you do not like?
4. If you were lost in the woods, what would you pray for?
5. What songs would you sing?
6. Give a chapter title for your life today.
7. Talk about a time when you were really happy.
8. Talk about a perfect day.
9. What were your parents' message to you about sex?
10. What were your parent's message to you about drugs and alcohol?

11. Talk about a hero of yours. Why are they so special?
12. Talk about something on your "bucket list." Why is it important?
13. Talk about something hanging on your refrigerator that is important to you.
14. How did you show kindness today?
15. What was a highlight of your day? What was a bad, sad, or least favorite time today?
16. List 5 things that you appreciate about your spouse.
17. What is the scariest thing that has ever happened to you?
18. Have you ever been hurt in love?
19. If you could give your younger self some advice, what would it be?
20. Name something that you need to forgive yourself for?
21. What kind of music do you listen to when you are sad?
22. What is the stupidest thing you've ever done?
23. What's the best thing that has ever happened to you?
24. If you wrote an autobiography, what would you call it?
25. What was one of your favorite birthdays and why?
26. Talk about a special event that was meaningful to you.
27. Talk about an important person in your life who has died.
28. Talk about some of your dreams for the future.

Appendix 4

Recipes for Family Living

THE IDEAS HERE are meant for families in trouble looking for help, successful families looking for new ideas, and families who want better approaches for those areas in their family life that need improvement. Just as the recipes in a cookbook give directions to help you make a certain dish, below is useful information that can be applied to improve the quality of your family life.

And just as there is more than one way to make a pot roast, there are many ways to achieve a happy family. So, choose the ingredients that are appropriate for you. Find ways to "spice up" your family and enjoy the rewards of a meal well made.

Bad habits: My parents were pretty creative in dealing with my sister and me and our sloppy, lazy natures. For example: my sister and I used to throw our coats on the floor after school instead of hanging them up in the closet. My parents started a collection jar for each violation. We had to contribute money into the jar each time we were caught with our coat on the floor. Not only did we change our habit quickly, but we also learned some values regarding money.

Bedtimes: Bedtimes were an issue in my childhood. I wanted to stay up as late as my big sis, and she thought that she had the right to stay up later than me. My engineer Dad came up with a plan after attending a businessman's conference on communications, decision-making, and getting staff cooperation. He sat down with my sister and me to explore the problem and work on some solutions. First, he asked us "Do you feel that it is reasonable to have some sort of bedtime limits for children?"

After my sister and I agreed with the idea of a scheduled bedtime, we each came up with our idea of what were reasonable bedtimes for children of all ages from the two-year-old down the block to my 18-year-old cousin, and for every age in between.

We proceeded to make a chart of the determined bedtimes created from averaging his recommended bedtime with my sister's and with mine. He then asked if we thought that those were reasonable bedtimes for each age. We agreed. Then he asked if we were able to accept them as our bedtimes. We agreed again.

There was flexibility allowed for watching an occasional evening TV show or attending a special activity. Time could be borrowed from one night to another. The system worked. My sister and I followed the crazy bedtime chart for many years. We looked forward to our next birthday when our bedtime would move up to a later time, for example from 8:17 to 8:32.

Dinner chores: Again, my sister and I tended to be lazy in helping out around the house. So, when we were in high school, my Dad created another chart, this time dealing with "who does the dishes"? We had an AFS (American Field Service) sister from Norway living with us that year so we had a pinwheel chart for three dinner chores: who sets the table, who clears it, and who fills the dishwasher. We rotated the wheel each week so that no one was bored doing the same chore and we had the option to swap chores if it was mutually agreed upon. It is useful when the responsibilities are clear, and when the child/teen is involved in setting up the plan.

Curfew: Setting realistic curfew times for your teens might be done in a similar manner as suggested for bedtimes. Talking with parents of their friends and getting a consensus will cut down on the "everyone else can do it" ploy that many teenagers use to imply that they are not getting the same degree of freedom as their peers. If you know the standards of their friends' parents, they can't mislead you. The rules and standards, however, are your family's standards, and do not have to be identical to any other family.

If something is important to you, discuss it with your teenagers. If something is really important to your teenagers, try to find a good compromise for everyone. Plan for some amount of flexibility for special occasions such as the prom, or a school-sponsored ski trip that will get back late and have a plan for calling home if the curfew plans change.

Should you wait up or not? Some parents wait up until their children get home, and others do not. While going to bed before they come home may imply trust, it can also be interpreted as a lack of concern and therefore a lack of love. It isn't important which you do, but it is important that your children know that you both love them and trust them. Teenagers often feel a lot of self-doubt.

Waiting up can be seen as a lack of trust. Some parents cannot go to sleep until they know that everyone is home safe and sound. They are frightened. If this is your case, make sure your child knows that it is not a lack of trust in them but your own fears. Your belief in them is very important to their sense of self-confidence.

Don't make your concern into a hassle for them that they will resent. Even when they have done something wrong, try to keep a cool head. You might want to tell them that you will discuss it in the morning. They might not sleep so well that night, but your anxiety over their late arrival will not be adding to the emotions of your discussion the next day.

When teenagers start going out at night, invariably there is some concern about what is an appropriate time to be home, what to do about special circumstances, what transportation is needed, if there will be drinking or drugs as part of the evening's "entertainment," whether to wait up for their return (and what to say if you do). It is a time when communication of feelings is important and anxieties can easily lead to misunderstandings.

One night... My Mom talks about an evening when I was about 14 years old. I went to a movie with a boy whom they had just met for the first time when he came to get me. We headed off to a 7 p.m. movie. When we did not return by my parent's bedtime they started to worry. Checking the movie schedule, adding time for a snack, and walking home, it was still later than it should be. As my Dad got out of his pajamas and into his clothes, the anxiety rose.

He was in the car, heading down the driveway and planning to drive the route to the movie theater when he saw my date and me walking down the road. He got out of the car and exploded. My date took off. I ran into the house with my chin trembling, and close to tears. My Dad rarely got mad so this was a big deal to me. My Mom asked why I was so late. I explained that the 7 o'clock movie was full, so we got something to eat, went to the next showing, and came directly home, only to be yelled at by "Daddy." As far as I was concerned, it was entirely uncalled for.

My Mom explained their fears for my welfare not knowing why I was delayed. They had no way to contact me as this was life before cell phones, and they were about to go to the police. My feelings and their feelings were both valid, but we knew we did not want to have such a misunderstanding again. After that experience I was good at calling from a pay phone if there were any changes in my plans. My parents in return tried to remember to "get the facts" before assuming the worst.

It is good to include children in seeking solutions to problems. Not only does it improve the parent-child relationship and build the self-esteem and confidence of the child, but they also are more apt to follow the plan instead of rebelling.

Teens and transportation: If your teen has a driving license, discuss the rules for use of the car. Should the cost of gas be shared? If the car is used by several people, how will it be determined who can use it and when? Perhaps a calendar could be used where it is indicated who will have the vehicle. If there is a special need at some time, it should be noted as soon as possible so there won't be last minute assumptions that the car will be available.

If your teen doesn't drive and needs some transportation, devise a fair way to share the task of getting them there and back. If there are older siblings in the house, you might make a deal: in return for use of the family car they would supply the transportation for younger brother and sisters. Just as in work related carpools, this may be an answer you can figure out with the parents of your teen's friends. Are there safe alternatives other than by car? Is there a bus, train, subway, cab, or ride share available? Is walking a safe and healthy option?

Allowance: An allowance for a child can be a very useful tool. It can serve as their first experience with money management. It helps them learn: to make choices, to plan ahead, how to save for things beyond their normal abilities, the consequences of buying impulsively, and it gives them a feeling of independence. An allowance can start at a very early age but should be scaled realistically to the needs it will serve. When allowance covers basic needs such as clothing, entertainment, travel expenses, and more it obviously must be much greater than if it just covers the desire for luxuries and the whims of the child or teen.

Needs and capabilities are to some degree age related. Certainly, I wouldn't expect a six-year-old to buy all of his or her own clothing. But it is realistic to think that a sixteen-year-old might. The responsibilities and size of an allowance can be increased in small steps, as the child gets older. Before starting to give out an allowance it is useful to sit down with your child and explain what is happening. Make it clear how much money they will receive, how long it will be before they will receive more, and what they are expected to cover with it.

As your child gets older it is reasonable to increase their allowance and therefore the ability to cover more expenses. It may start with entertainment expenses such as video games or going to the movies, gifts for friends and family members, make-up and jewelry, or other hobbies and interests. Allowance money for clothing obligations should start with less significant items such as fun socks, colorful stockings, or scarves, and then add shoes, shirts, and jeans as they get more mature and can handle more financial responsibility.

When our children were young, I wanted to give them an allowance so that they would learn about money management and have some decision-making skills when it came to spending money on fun things. I decided to check in with them every Friday so that they could self-evaluate how they did for the week. I gave them one dollar if they said they thought they keep their room decently picked up, and one dollar if they were basically kind people. Not only did they learn about money, but also, I reinforced values that were important to me.

Frustration-Impatience: Here's another story from my childhood. One day I got very upset because I had to go to the bathroom immediately after my sister had gone and I tried to flush the toilet before the tank had refilled. Outraged and teary, I protested to my father, "The toilet broke!" Calmly my father explained to me, "But you haven't done the magic thing!" Immediately intrigued enough to forget about my frustration, I enquired what he meant. "Well, you haven't touched all the doorknobs in the house. If you do that, I'm sure the toilet will flush."

I proceeded to run around the house, touching all of the doorknobs, and then went to the toilet and VOILA—it worked. For years I used the same method whenever the situation repeated itself, never feeling that same frustration again because I was in control; I knew the magic answer. Still to this day I might be caught running around my parents' house touching doorknobs with a twinkle in my eye and a skip in my stride. Sometimes it is not easy to think up clever tactics, but when you do and they work, they become a special family memory.

Appendix 5

A Story of Spirituality

I WANT TO share a personal story of mine that I think is particularly interesting and powerful. It involves family, wedding rings, and faith in a higher power. I love when life events seem magical and divinely influenced. How else can it be explained? Enjoy!

Back in 1989 my cousin Helene came to visit Israel and me. At that time, we were busy studying Judaism and spirituality of all kinds. Knowing Helene was a devout Christian, I decided to ask her to give me some examples of spirituality and faith from her life's experience. I didn't know the biggest lesson in spirituality was yet to come.

Helene told me about a course she had attended, in hopes of improving her marriage. As part of the course, she listed her heart's desires, then sifted through her list using a biblical process to produce four distinct lists: one to pray on, one to pray and act on, one to pray and get information on, and one and to pray and wait on God when the path was not quite clear.

One of the things that ended up on her "pray and wait" list was a diamond engagement ring for her 20th anniversary. She had a wedding ring but never had an engagement ring and she wanted one that was truly meaningful to her. She tried to get her husband excited about the idea several times, but that wasn't happening. So, she went about following her spiritual path and letting God know about her desires and "waiting for Him to take care of it in His time and in His way."

As she shared her story with me it was clear to me what I needed to do. I was in possession of a diamond engagement ring that belonged to our grandmother, also named Helene. It was from a Latin American suitor of hers, not our grandfather. My cousin's husband is also Latin American, believe it or not. I had worn the ring briefly during my engagement to my first husband, but for years it had been sitting in my jewelry box.

As I handed the ring to my cousin, she was stunned and in awe of how her faith, trust, and belief in God's promises got her something that she never imagined she would get, and in a way that was unforeseeable.

Twenty years later, Helene decided that she wanted a new wedding band to match her engagement ring. Several months passed when she was looking for a parking space in a crowded area. As she pulled in and looked up, she saw a sign, "Going Out of Business—everything 80% off."

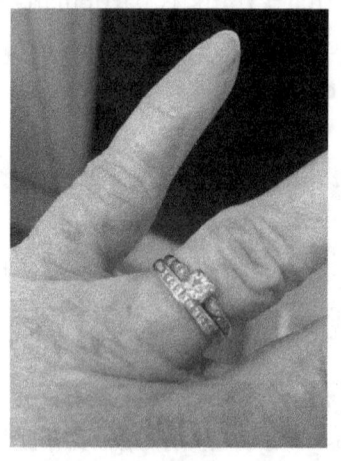

Helene went in to look around and told the lady her story. The clerk said she hoped she had the right ring for her, but they were only selling what was left there—no special orders. When they started looking in the case, they found only one ring that seemed right, and it happened to fit perfectly. She found a perfect new wedding band to match the engagement ring, at exactly her budget. It was simply meant to be!

Appendix 6

Books and Other Resources

If you are looking for therapy:

Our retreat websites: https://marriagequest.org
https://sexploration.org
Our son, Dr David Helfand: https://lifewisevt.com/private-retreats/
Marriage or family counseling: https://aamft.org
Sex therapy: https://aasect.org (not .com)
Individual therapy: https://psychologytoday.com
Neurofeedback-biofeedback:
https://lifewisevt.com
https://isnr.org
https://bcia.org
https://aapb.org
For Trauma/PTSD: https://emdr.com

Group workshops:

https://mankindproject.org Mankind Project/New Warrior weekend workshops
https://womanwithin.org Woman Within weekend workshops

https://hoffmaninstitute.org 7-Day retreats for transformative healing
https://www1.hai.org Weekend workshops for Love, Intimacy, and Sexuality

Sex websites and products:

https://www.omgyes.com/ Research based info for women and orgasm (a paid site)
https://evelynresh.com/ Evelyn Resh RN is a good resource for sexual goals and medication balance.
https://missjaiya.com/ Take the quiz to understand your "erotic blueprint"
https://badgirlsbible.com/ for sexual techniques, dirty talk, and more. Some free ideas and some for a fee.
https://www.babeland.com/ For adult/sex toys.
Vibrators for the orgasm challenged: Wahl electric. Jimmy Jane battery.

Lubes for sex:

Pjur Bodyglide, Eros, or Wet lubricant (black bottles - silicone, not for toys).
ID Glide is good water-based lube
Kama Sutra oil from Youthing Strategies. http://youthingstrategies.com/
Some women like coconut oil
https://aloecadabra.com/ Lube for oral sex (no dyes; vanilla is great)
Lubes for restoring balance (for itchy or smelly times)
    https://goodcleanlove.com/ (Restore)
    https://vmagicnow.com/ (V Magic)

Some book suggestions:

Marriage:

The Five Love Languages: The Secret to Love That Lasts – Gary Chapman
Mating in Captivity: Unlocking Erotic Intelligence – Esther Perel
Couple Skills: Making Your Relationship Work – McKay, Fanning & Paleg
Why Marriages Succeed or Fail: And How You Can Make Yours Last – John Gottman

The Unresolved Dispute: There's Hope for Your Marriage – Rev. Gilbert Coleman, Jr. (Christian)
Relationship Transformation: Have Your Cake and Eat It Too – Jerry Duberstein and Mary Ellen Goggin
101 Things I Wish I Knew When I Got Married: Simple Lessons To Make Love Last – Linda and Charlie Bloom
Passionate Marriage: Keeping Love Alive in Committed Relationships – David Schnarch, Ph.D.
A Celebration of Marriage – Rabbi Alan Green (Jewish)
Married People – Francine Klagsbrun
The Highly Sensitive Person in Love – Elaine N. Aron
Intimate Partners: Patterns in Love and Marriage – Maggie Scarf
For Better: The Science of a Good Marriage – Tara Parker-Pope
Successful Second Marriages – Patricia Bubash
Do I Have to Give Up Me To Be Loved By You? – Jordan and Margaret Paul
The Angry Marriage – Bonnie Maslin
The Art of Loving – Erich Fromm
The Mastery of Love – Don Miguel Ruiz
Romantic Intelligence – Valentis and Valentis
Men, Women and the Power of Empathy – A.R. Maslow

Sex:

The Guide to Getting It On – Paul Joannides
Come as You Are: The Surprising New Science That Will Transform Your Sex Life – Emily Nagoski
I ♥ Female Orgasms: An Extrordinary Orgasm Guide – Dorian Solat and Marshall Miller
Read My Lips: A Complete Guide to the Vagina and Vulva – Debby Herbenick and Vanessa Schick
The Complete Manual of Sexual Positions – Jessica Stewart
Hot Monogamy – Love and Robinson

Lovelight: Unveiling the Mysteries of Sex and Romance – Julia Bondi

Rekindling Desire: A Step by Step Program to Help Low-Sex and No-Sex Marriages – Barry and Emily McCarthy

Enduring Desire: Your Guide to Lifelong Intimacy – Metz and McCarthy

The New Joy of Sex – Alex Comfort

Arousal: The Secret Logic of Sexual Fantasies – Michael Bader

The Better Sex Guide: How to Maintain a Healthy Sex Life in a Loving Relationship – Nitya Lacroix

The Big Book of Masturbation: From Angst to Zeal – Martha Cornog

Sex Over 50 – Joel Block

Your Brain on Sex: How Smarter Sex Can Change Your Life – Stanley Siegel

The Erotic Mind: Unlocking the Inner Sources of Sexual Passion & Fulfillment – Jack Morin

DVD – The Tantric Secrets of Sacred Sex: A Guide to Intimacy & Loving

Affairs:

After the Affair: Healing the Pain and Rebuilding Trust When a Partner Has Been Unfaithful – Janis Abrahms Spring

How Can I Forgive You – Janis Abrahms Spring

Divorce:

Rebuilding: When Your Relationship Ends – Dr. Bruce Fisher

The Divorce Book – McKay, Rogers, Blades, and Gosse

Learning to Love Again – Mel Krantzler

Creative Divorce: A New Opportunity for Personal Growth – Mel Krantzler

Women:

Transformation Through Menopause – Marian VanEyk McCain

The Heroines' Journey – Maureen Murdock

Real Sex for Real Women – Laura Berman

The Wisdom of Menopause – Christiane Northrup

The 30-Day Natural Hormone Plan – Erika Schwartz

Our Bodies Ourselves – Boston Women's Health Collective

I'm Not in The Mood: What Every Woman Should Know About Improving her Libido – Judith Reichman

Passages: Predictable Crises of Adult Life – Gail Sheehy

Men:

Hazards of Being Male – Herb Goldberg

Finding Our Fathers – Samuel Osherson

King, Warrior, Magician, Lover – Gillette and Moore

The Flying Boy: Healing the Wounded Man – John Lee

Fire in the Belly: On Being a Man – Sam Keen

A Little Book on The Human Shadow – Robert Bly

The Seasons of a Man's Life – Daniel J. Levinson

You Can Beat Prostate Cancer: And You Don't Need Surgery to Do It – Robert Marckini

Personal Growth:

Self-Parenting: A Guide to Inner Conversations – John Pollard (workbook)

Meeting Yourself Halfway: 31 Value Clarification Strategies for Daily Living – Sidney Simon (workbook)

Values Clarification – Simon, Howe, Kirschenbaum

Choose the Life You Want: The Mindful Way to Happiness – Tal Ben-Shahar

Happier – Tal Ben-Shahar

The 7 Habits of Highly Effective People – Stephen Covey

The Winner's Notebook – Theodore Isaac Rubin

The Dance of Anger – Harriet Lerner

Fear and Other Uninvited Guests – Harriet Lerner

The Way of the Peaceful Warrior – Dan Millman

The Road Less Traveled – M. Scott Peck

The Mystic Path to Cosmic Power – Vernon Howard

The Four Agreements – Don Miguel Ruiz

Transitions: Making Sense of Life's Changes – William Bridges

When Anger Hurts: Quieting the Storm Within – McKay, Rogers, and McKay
When All You've Ever Wanted is Not Enough – Harold Kushner
Your Perfect Right: A Guide to Assertive Living – Alberti and Emmons
Money Harmony – Olivia Mellan
Getting to Yes: Negotiating Agreement Without Giving In – Fisher and Ury
Born to Win – Muriel James
Pulling Your Own Strings – Wayne Dyer
Man's Search for Himself – Rollo May
The Power of Positive Thinking – Norman Vincent Peale
All I Really Need to Know I Learned in Kindergarten – Robert Fulghum
The Laws of Spirit: A Tale of Transformation – Dan Millman
On Death and Dying – Elisabeth Kubler-Ross
Death: The Final Stage – Elisabeth Kubler-Ross
Talking About Death – Virginia Morris
The Conversation – Angelo Volandes (talking about plans for your death)
Being Mortal – Atul Gawande

Body/Mind Healing:

The Power of Focusing: Practical Guide to Emotional Self-Healing – Cornell
A Mindfulness-Based Stress Reduction Workbook – Stahl and Goldstein
Focusing – Eugene Gendlin
Minding the Body, Mending the Mind – Joan Borysenko
Stress Breakers – Helene Lerner
In Search of Balance – Robbins and Mortifee
Don't Sweat the Small Stuff – Michael Mantell
The Power of Personal Health – Jack Schwartz
Ayurvedic Healing – Candis Cantin Packard
Heal Your Body – Louise L. Hay
How to Meditate – Lawrence LeShan
The Lazy Man's Guide to Enlightenment – Thaddeus Golas
Sugar Blues – William Duffy
Food: What the Heck Should I Eat – Mark Hyman

Spirituality:

What is God? – Etan Boritzer (great for kids and adults)
The First Step – Rebbe Zalman Shachter-Shalomi
If You Meet the Buddha on the Road, Kill Him – Sheldon Kopp
Voices of Wisdom: Jewish Ideals and Ethics for Everyday Living – Francine Klagsbrun
When Bad Things Happen to Good People – Harold Kushner
Chop Wood, Carry Water – Editors of New Age Journal
As Above, So Below – Ron Miller and the editors of New Age Journal
Dawn – Elie Wiesel
Night – Elie Wiesel
Medicine Cards (great cards for self-discovery)
Jewish Meditation – Aryeh Kaplan
Peace at Every Step – Thich Nhat Hanh
The Seat of the Soul – Gary Zukav
I and Thou – Martin Buber (Classic Existentialism)
Other Lives, Other Selves – Roger Woolger (Past Lives)
The Prophet – Kahlil Gibran
The Personal Totem Pole – Eligio Stephen Gallegos
Seven Ways to Look at a Dream – Margot Born (Senoi, Dream Theater, Body Techniques, Freud, Jung, Gestalt, Problem Solving)
The Seven Spiritual Laws of Success: A Practical Guide to the Fulfillment of Your Dreams – Deepak Chopra

Addictions & Co-Dependency:

The Myth of Sex Addiction – David Ley
The Better Way to Drink – Vogler and Bartz
From Chocolate to Morphine – Andrew Weil (A balanced book, not scare tactics)
Sex, Drugs, Gambling & Chocolate: A Workbook for Overcoming Addictions – A. Thomas Horvath
The Sober Truth: Debunking the Bad Science Behind 12-step Programs and the Rehab Industry – Lance Dodes and Zachary Dodes

Marijuana is Safer: So why are we driving people to drink? – Fox, Armentano, Tvert
A Workbook for Healing – Patty McConnell (ACOA)
Fat is a Family Affair – Judi Hollis
Compulsive Eaters and Relationships – Matsakis Aphrodite
A Substance Called Food – Gloria Arenson
The Intimacy Struggle – Janet Woititz
Choice Making for Co-Dependents, Adult Children and Spirituality Seekers – Sharon Wegscheider-Cruse

Lifework Direction:

Synchronicity: The Inner Path of Leadership – Joseph Jaworski
Hope for the Flowers – Trina Paulus (great for all ages)
The Corporate Mystic – Gay Hendricks
The Living Company: Habits for Survival in a Turbulent Business Environment – Arie de Geus
The Fifth Discipline: The Art and Practice of The Learning Organization – Peter Senge
The Reinvention of Work: A New Vision of Livelihood in Our Time – Matthew Fox
What Should I Do with My Life – PO Bronson
How to Change the World: Social Entrepreneurs and the Power of New Ideas – David Bornstein

Family Systems/Parenting:

The Ungame – a game about feelings for young children – good cards are available for older children and couples
Parenting – Louise Guerney (NIRE.org) Matches the communications that we use.
Liking Myself – Pat Palmer (self-esteem building for children ages 5-9)
The Mouse, The Monster, and Me – Pat Palmer (self-esteem building for children ages 8-12)

The New Peoplemaking – Virginia Satir
Raising Cain – Daniel Kindlon (raising a son)
It's Perfectly Normal – Robie Harris (sex book for children/adolescents)
50 Wonderful Ways to be a Single-Parent Family – Barry G. Ginsberg
How to Behave So Your Children Will, Too! – Sal Severe
Stepmonster: A New Look at Why Real Stepmothers Think, Feel, and Act the Way We Do – Wednesday Martin

Mental and Physical Health:

Stop Walking on Eggshells: Taking Your Life Back When Someone You Care About Has Borderline Personality Disorder – Mason & Kreger
I Hate You-Don't Leave Me: Understanding the Borderline Personality – Jerold J. Kreisman
Borderline Personality Disorder: Struggling, Understanding, Succeeding (written for professionals) – Colleen Warner
When Husbands Come Out of the Closet – Jean Schaar Gochros
Allies in Healing – Laura Davis (for sexual childhood abuse)
Courage to Heal Workbook: Overcoming Childhood Sexual Abuse – Laura Davis

Acknowledgements

A SPECIAL THANKS to Israel, my husband, co-therapist, co-parent, boss, playmate, and partner on this journey who encouraged me to write and re-write this YUMMY book. And thanks for all of his work on his dissertation, *Marital Conservation*—the basis of some of this information.

My parents, Jerry and Clare Worthing, who tirelessly helped with editing YUMMY, gave lots of support, and were role models in approaching a huge writing project like this. My sister, Joan, who was my childhood playmate and awesome travel buddy. Perry Woods for all of his amazing artwork, and our lifelong friendship. Dana Treidel who shared many conversations with me on sex and marriage.

Thanks to the late Kenneth F. Mutch who taught me about what I want and don't want in a marriage. Dr. Claire Lehr who started me on my path to being a marriage counselor many years ago at Ohio Wesleyan University. Mary Ellen Goggin who gave me great resources for editing and publishing. My talented and patient editor and word shaper, Helena Kaufman. Kelly Burch for some great developmental edits. My cousin, Susie Wyshak, for her helpful editing suggestions. Bublish for their great layout team. Mary Armstrong and Cheryl McMahon for being my office buddies.

And finally, a big thank you to Amanda for hours of line editing, emotional support, and being a creative spark to me. And to David for taking our life's work into the future. I'm excited to see how it continues to evolve.

We have created an eclectic and unique process based on the work of many teachers, trainers, and mentors over the years. Our work is enhanced by our own marriage and life experiences. Predominantly we draw from the Family Systems Theory work of Virginia Satir; Differentiation concepts from Murray Bowen; Rational Emotive Therapy from Albert Ellis; Relationship Enhancement Training from Bernard Guerney and Barry Ginsberg; Psychodrama from J.L. Moreno and many of his students; the Co-dependency work of Sharon Wegsheider-Cruse; research on successful marriages from the Gottman Institute; creative perspectives on affairs and intimacy from Esther Perel; and the creative interventions ideas of many strategic family therapy trainers.

Spiritual subtleties come from years of studying energy work, rituals, and Rites of Passage work with gurus such as Jack Schwartz, Steven Foster and Meredith Little, and Rabbi Zalman Schachter-Shalomi.

About the Authors

CATHIE AND ISRAEL Helfand have been working together with couples for more than 35 years. They run Marriage Quest and Sexploration retreat programs at their 1850s homestead in Northern Vermont, where they have welcomed couples from around the world.

As a married couple, they have first-hand experience in dealing with the challenges and benefits of a modern married life. Their work has been described as warp-speed therapy and ass-kicking. It is often intense as well as transformative.

The Helfand's have helped thousands of couples deal with their decision of staying in the marriage or getting a divorce. Most couples want to learn how to communicate in healthier ways, and how to have a YUMMY marriage. Cathie and Israel are pro-marriage but not at any cost. Some people are happier, and will be healthier, if they let go of the marriage and move on with skills for a new beginning.

Donations to our educational non-profit are appreciated so we can donate books to libraries, VA Centers, and other non-profits as well as offer retreats to Veterans who cannot afford our services.

All Seasons VT, Inc
340 Deeper Ruts Rd
Cabot VT 05647
helfand@marriagequest.org

www.ingramcontent.com/pod-product-compliance
Lightning Source LLC
Chambersburg PA
CBHW052204090526
44583CB00015BA/1497